O9-BTN-157

What Does It Mean to Be Chosen?

The CHOSEN

An Interactive Bible Study

Season 1

What Does It Mean to Be Chosen?

Amanda Jenkins, Dallas Jenkins, & Douglas S. Huffman

DAVID C COOK

transforming lives together

WHAT DOES IT MEAN TO BE CHOSEN?
Published by David C Cook
4050 Lee Vance Drive
Colorado Springs, CO 80918 U.S.A.

Integrity Music Limited, a Division of David C Cook
Brighton, East Sussex BN1 2RE, England

The graphic circle C logo is a registered trademark of David C Cook.

All rights reserved. Except for brief excerpts for review purposes,
no part of this book may be reproduced or used in any form
without written permission from the publisher.

The website addresses recommended throughout this book are offered as a resource
to you. These websites are not intended in any way to be or imply an endorsement
on the part of David C Cook, nor do we vouch for their content.

All Scripture quotations are taken from the ESV® Bible (The Holy Bible, English Standard Version®), copyright
© 2001 by Crossway, a publishing ministry of Good News Publishers. Used by permission. All rights
reserved. The authors have added italics, underline, and larger type to Scripture quotations for emphasis.

ISBN 978-0-8307-8268-0
eISBN 978-0-8307-8269-7

© 2021 The Chosen, LLC

The Team: Michael Covington, Stephanie Bennett, Jack Campbell, Susan Murdock
Cover Design: James Hershberger

Printed in the United States of America
First Edition 2021

5 6 7 8 9 10 11 12 13 14

042021

CONTENTS

PREFACE

We're guessing this Bible study will be unlike others you've encountered. Most studies that include video content are lecture based with teaching centered on a specific topic or portion of Scripture. This Bible study, however, is designed to be used in conjunction with *The Chosen*, the groundbreaking streaming television series about the life of Jesus. Each session works in tandem with an episode from the show, bringing the Old and New Testaments to life in a fresh way.

To get the most out of the show and the content we've compiled, we have a few suggestions and some people for you to meet. These characters will function as our proxies, pulling us into the story of Jesus and helping us uncover more of our own stories.

But more on that in a minute.

Who Is This Study For?

You.

And us.

Because whether you're just starting out on the Jesus road or you're decades along, being chosen has far-reaching ramifications and endless applications—especially in a day and age when issues of identity are at the forefront of culture, and insecurity, confusion, and a desire for purpose seem to reign supreme.

How Should It Be Used?

Both/And

This study has been designed for small groups who want unique content and good discussion, but it works just as well for individual study. In either case, each lesson's corresponding episode should be viewed *before* going through the material.

Wrap-up

You will end each lesson with a "Prayer Focus" as well as "Further Study" suggestions that can be used throughout the week to go even deeper into Scripture.

Discussion Questions

Each lesson features ten questions that will take you from an introductory level, to an exploratory level, to an engagement level, to an application level.

So many levels.

Scripture Citations

The Bible verses in this study are taken from the English Standard Version. The ESV is an up-to-date translation aiming at word-for-word formal equivalency—which is a fancy way of saying it's an excellent resource for carefully studying the words of Scripture. But regardless of the Bible translation you use, we encourage you to gain more context by looking up the recommended verses for yourself.

Helpful Stuff to Know

If there's an abbreviation, word, or phrase you don't understand, take a look in the margins where we've translated most of our Christianese.

Helpful Stuff to See

We've included an Old Testament Timeline as well as a couple of maps to help you visualize the big picture. They're really cool.

Timeline of Biblical Events in World History Context

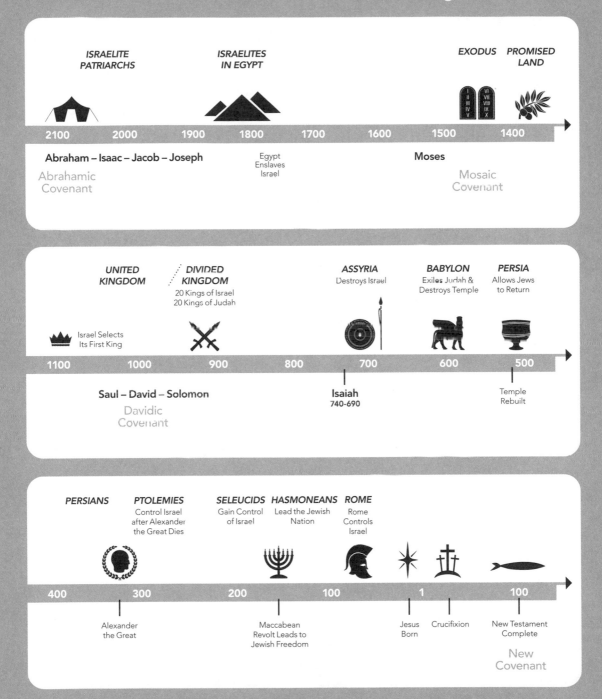

ISRAELITE PATRIARCHS

ISRAELITES IN EGYPT

EXODUS | **PROMISED LAND**

2100 | 2000 | 1900 | 1800 | 1700 | 1600 | 1500 | 1400

Abraham – Isaac – Jacob – Joseph

Egypt Enslaves Israel

Moses

Abrahamic Covenant

Mosaic Covenant

UNITED KINGDOM

DIVIDED KINGDOM
20 Kings of Israel
20 Kings of Judah

ASSYRIA
Destroys Israel

BABYLON
Exiles Judah & Destroys Temple

PERSIA
Allows Jews to Return

Israel Selects Its First King

1100 | 1000 | 900 | 800 | 700 | 600 | 500

Saul – David – Solomon

Isaiah
740-690

Temple Rebuilt

Davidic Covenant

PERSIANS

PTOLEMIES
Control Israel after Alexander the Great Dies

SELEUCIDS
Gain Control of Israel

HASMONEANS
Lead the Jewish Nation

ROME
Rome Controls Israel

400 | 300 | 200 | 100 | 1 | 100

Alexander the Great

Maccabean Revolt Leads to Jewish Freedom

Jesus Born

Crucifixion

New Testament Complete

New Covenant

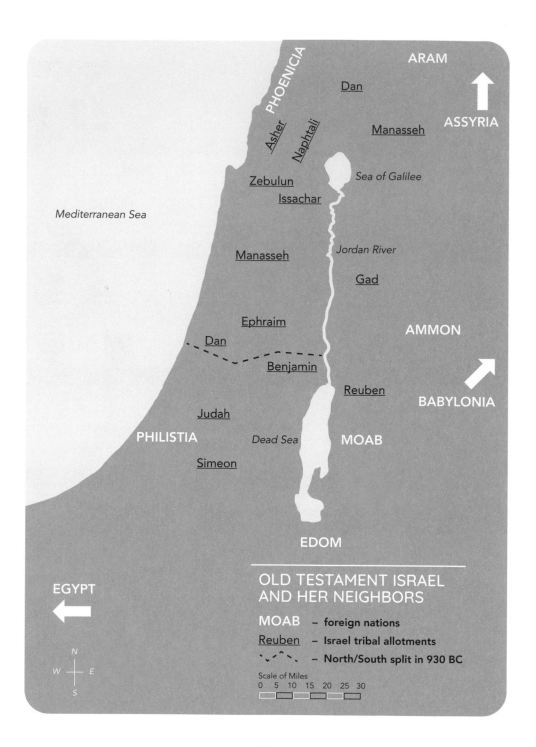

ARAM

PHOENICIA

Dan

ASSYRIA

Asher Naphtali

Manasseh

Zebulun

Sea of Galilee

Issachar

Mediterranean Sea

Manasseh

Jordan River

Gad

Ephraim

AMMON

Dan

Benjamin

Reuben

BABYLONIA

Judah

PHILISTIA

Dead Sea

MOAB

Simeon

EDOM

EGYPT

OLD TESTAMENT ISRAEL AND HER NEIGHBORS

MOAB – foreign nations

<u>Reuben</u> – Israel tribal allotments

–·–·– – North/South split in 930 BC

Scale of Miles

0 5 10 15 20 25 30

N W E S

Sidon •

ABILENE

Mt. Hermon
^

Tyre •

PHOENICIA

Caesarea Philippi •

Ituraea   Trachonitis

Batanaea

Lake Semechonitis

GALILEE

GAULANITIS

Ptolemais •

Capernaum •   • Bethsaida

Auranitis

• Cana   • Gerasa

Sepphoris •

Sea of Galilee

Mt. Carmel ^

Tiberias •

Nazareth • Mt. Tabor ^   • Gadara

Mediterranean Sea

Nain •

DECAPOLIS

Caesarea •

Scythopolis •

Jordan River

Sebaste/Samaria •

• Gerasa

Mt. Gerizim
^

Antipatris •

SAMARIA

PEREA

Joppa •

Philadelphia •

• Arimathea

• Lydda   Jericho •

Jerusalem • • Bethany   • Madaba

Bethlehem •

Azotus •   • Qumran

Ascalon •

JUDEA

• Machaerus

Gaza •   Hebron •

Dead Sea

IDUMEA   En Gedi •

Masada •

Beersheba •   • Charachmoba

NABATEA

NABATEA

ISRAEL IN NEW
TESTAMENT TIMES

GALILEE – geo-political regions

Caesarea • – cities

Scale of Miles
0   5   10   15   20   25   30

N
W ——+—— E
S

MEET THE MAINS

Mary Magdalene

"… Mary, called Magdalene, from whom seven demons had gone out …"

Luke 8:2

With so many women in the Bible named Mary, this one was distinguished by her hometown of Magdala—one of several fishing villages on the Sea of Galilee. What we know of her from the New Testament (NT) is that prior to meeting Jesus, she was a tormented woman, possessed by seven demons. Side note: "Lilith" was Mary's alias in episode 1, which derives from an ancient Middle Eastern term for "female demons" or "wind spirits." Only Jesus was able to drive them out, and Mary of Magdala became one of His devoted followers.

In a culture that viewed women as less valuable than men, Mary became a significant member of the team.

1. She was among the female disciples who traveled with Jesus and financially supported His ministry (Luke 8:1–3).
2. She was present at His crucifixion and burial (Matt. 27:56–61).
3. She was the first to witness the empty tomb (John 20:1) and meet the resurrected Jesus (John 20:11–18; Matt. 28:1; Mark 16:1–6).

And she got to tell the boys.

Nicodemus

"Now there was a man of the Pharisees named Nicodemus, a ruler of the Jews."

John 3:1

There were different factions within Judaism:

Pharisees:
scholars who interpreted the law to the masses, along with oral traditions. Connected to the local synagogues and highly respected by the common people. Believed in the afterlife.

Sadducees:
the professional religious aristocracy connected to the temple, committed to the written law alone. They were resigned to submit to Roman rule. Did not believe in the afterlife.

Essenes:
separatists who lived in various communes that were focused on prayer, holy living, and the future. Not directly mentioned in the New Testament.

Zealots:
political activists organized to rebel against Rome and against Jewish leaders who cooperated with Rome.

Nicodemus was a leading Pharisee in first-century Judaism and a member of the Sanhedrin, the ruling council of the Jews (John 3:1). As a spiritual leader, he had influence in all areas of society since Israel's religious system determined the laws of the land politically, culturally, and socially. Pharisees were well-respected, theologically conservative believers in God and His Word, often laypeople devoted to pure living and worship in the local synagogue. On the other hand, priests who were connected to the official worship practices of the Jerusalem temple were more likely to be members of the Sadducee party and were typically in league with Roman rule—which is why Quintus (the fictional Roman leader who interacts with Nicodemus in episode 1) comments on the Sadducees being the enemies of the Pharisees (Acts 23:1–10).

While most of the religious leaders denied Jesus's claim to be the Son of God, Nicodemus was among the few men of influence to admit what His miracles and otherworldly teaching meant: Jesus came from God (John 3:2).

Matthew

"As Jesus passed on from there, he saw a man called Matthew sitting at the tax booth."

Matthew 9:9

Matthew was also known by his Hebrew name, Levi (Mark 2:14; Luke 5:27). He collected taxes on behalf of the Roman Empire, which made him a traitor to his fellow Jews. He seemed indifferent to their suffering as well as to the demise of his relationships and his reputation.

Matthew's collection booth was located in the Galilean town of Capernaum, which was the birthplace of Jesus's ministry. Coming face to face with the miracle-man-preacher obliterated Matthew's loyalty to Rome and his apathy toward others. He subsequently became one of Jesus's disciples, author of the first book of the New Testament, and a faithful follower for the rest of his life (Matt. 10:3).

Simon (a.k.a., Simon Peter)

"While walking by the Sea of Galilee, [Jesus] saw two brothers, Simon (who is called Peter) and Andrew his brother, casting a net into the sea, for they were fishermen."

Matthew 4:18

We know that Simon Peter lived in Capernaum (Mark 1:21–29), where he was a fisherman with his brother

Andrew (Matt. 4:18; Mark 1:16), and that he was married (Matt. 8:14; Mark 1:30; Luke 4:38). Simon is described in the New Testament as being an overly confident man who seemed to think he could earn his worth and who sometimes spoke with little forethought (Matt. 16:21–23; 26:31–35, 69–75). Luke's gospel actually makes note of one such moment, remarking after a statement made by Simon, "not knowing what he said" (Luke 9:33).

Regardless, Jesus still called this man to follow Him (Luke 5:1–11) and was patient with him (Luke 22:31–32). Simon Peter became a key leader among the twelve apostles (Acts 1–12), bedrock preacher of the early church (Matt. 16:18), writer of two New Testament books of the Bible (1 and 2 Pet.), healer of the sick and lame (Acts 5:15), and fearless unto death (John 21:15–19).

While intimately connected to *The Chosen* TV series, we hope our character-based approach in this Bible study will get readers more deeply connected to Jesus. After all, Jesus—the One foretold in the Old Testament and affirmed in the New—is the One doing the choosing. And when we see Him through the eyes of those who actually met Him—the people He called while ministering on earth—we can be changed and impacted in the same way they were.

Which begs the question: What does it mean to be chosen?

Amanda Jenkins, Dallas Jenkins, and Doug Huffman

INTRODUCTION

Old and New

Why study a passage from the book of Isaiah in the Old Testament when the life of Jesus is covered in the New Testament? Good question. **Because what we call "Old" was the only Bible Jesus ever used!** In fact, the New Testament hadn't even been written when Jesus was on earth, because it's the testimony of His life—and the lives of His chosen followers.

Naturally, the television series *The Chosen* draws from the four Gospels of the New Testament. But it's noteworthy how often the show makes reference to the Old—in quotes, allusions, or flashbacks—because the story of Jesus and humanity's deep-seated need for Him began at creation (Gen. 3:15). And so, the intertwining story threads from the Old Testament to the New Testament are intricate and profound—and also cool.

In fact, God's chosen nation of Israel is important Old Testament background for what Jesus was doing when He chose His followers in the New Testament. For example, out of His many followers called "disciples," Jesus selected twelve to be leaders, whom He called "apostles" (Luke

Old Testament (OT): the first major section of the Bible, it is the testimony of God's relationship with the nation of Israel and His preparation of salvation for all humanity, written by His representatives among the ancient people of God.

New Testament (NT): the second major section of the Bible, it is the testimony of Jesus's life and its implications for all humanity, written by those who knew Him best.

"Disciples" of Jesus are people devoted to following Him, and Jesus had crowds of disciples during His earthly ministry (and millions of them since!).

"Apostles" were twelve of Jesus's disciples whom He selected to be leaders among the rest of His disciples.

6:12–17). The number *twelve* echoes the twelve tribes of Old Testament Israel and serves as a clear indication of Jesus's intentions to reestablish the people of God.

And there's plenty more where that came from—**countless points of continuity** between the Old Testament and the New Testament. But let's not get ahead of ourselves.

The story of Israel is one of great drama that includes adventures and explorations, successes and failures, romances and rebellions, wars and disasters, devastations and rescues. Consider this speech from Simon in episode 4. While it comes from a place of anger, frustration, and desperation—and the blame is misplaced—he isn't wrong on the history:

> "And I will make your descendants as numerous as the stars in the heavens …" And then what, huh? Make the chosen as many as the stars, only to let Egypt enslave us for generations? Bring us out of Egypt, part the Red Sea, only to let us wander in the desert for forty years? Give us the land only to exile us in Babylon? Bring us back only to be crushed by Rome? This is the God I've served faithfully my whole life?! You're the God I'm supposed to thank? If I didn't know any better, I'd say You enjoy yanking us around like goats and can't decide whether we're chosen or not. Which is it, huh?!

A more accurate way to put it? God rescued Israel again and again, in spite of their constant rebellion against Him. They sinned their way into slavery (Egypt) and suffering (the wilderness) and exile (Babylon). And each time, God's rescue served as a reminder that they were His beloved, chosen people. They were repeatedly forgiven and restored, set apart and protected, provided for and loved, daily led on earth and assured of spending eternity with Him in heaven.

They were **chosen**.

What Simon didn't realize was that he and his people were about to be rescued again. Not in the way they expected, but in a way that would radically and permanently change their lives—along with the whole wide world. Because bound up in God's proven faithfulness to Israel are prophecies and promises about a coming Messiah that would extend the status of "chosen" to all who respond to His call.

Messiah: the promised deliverer of the Jewish nation (or, "Savior").

That's us. **We're the chosen people of God**.

The series title, *The Chosen*, refers to multiple things, including God's chosen nation of Israel and all those whom Jesus chooses. But what does it *actually* mean to be chosen? To answer that question, we're going Old school—Testament, that is. Which will lead us back to the New.

Which will lead us directly to Jesus.

Your Turn

1. How familiar are you with the Bible and its two major divisions: the Old Testament and the New Testament? What, if anything, do you think of or expect from them?

2. What do you know about the **connections** between the Old and New Testaments? How does Jesus factor into those connections? (Spoiler alert: read Luke 24:44.)

3. How much of the Bible have you actually read? What part(s) are you most attracted to, and why? What part(s) do you avoid, and why?

4. What comes to mind when you hear the words "chosen by God"? Do you find the notion comforting? Confusing? Merciful? Unfair? Life-giving?

How about all of the above and then some?

OT Context

The well-known story of Moses, the Israelites, and their exodus from Egypt is actually one that's been on repeat since the beginning of time. Not the plagues part. Or the parting of the Red Sea part. Or the walking through the wilderness for forty years part. Those mind-blowing details are unique to that time and place in history. But mankind's propensity to choose sin over God's purpose and plan has remained firmly in place since the Garden of Eden.

It goes like this:

The Sin Cycle

God's Plan
is good and awesome and
loving and for our good and
His glory.

We sin
and go our own way.
Again.

We deviate
from God's plan by
sinning and going our
own way.

We receive forgiveness
and our relationship with God
is restored. We renew our
commitment to surrender
to God's plan.

We need to be rescued
from sin and the consequences
of our own bad choices
(which are not good or awesome
or loving or for our good
or His glory).

We repent
from our sin and God is willing,
able, and faithful to forgive us
and rescue us.

And on it goes. In story after story from the Old Testament, we see that pattern play out, and the circumstances around the writing of the book of Isaiah were no different. Once again, the Israelites were in a sin cycle. God rescued their ancestors from Pharaoh and led them through the wilderness with a cloud by day and a pillar of fire by night (Ex. 13:21)—which meant He was the map. He fed them; every day food appeared on the ground, and also water came from rocks (Ex. 16:4–5; Num. 20:7–8). God conquered armies that stood in Israel's way and established them in the land He'd promised them (Josh. 1–24). All the while, generation after generation grumbled and complained and disobeyed the God who chose them. They made demands and changed God's plans, and everything got progressively worse.

Enter Isaiah.

We don't actually know a ton about the prophet Isaiah. The OT book that bears his name begins with this introduction: "The vision of Isaiah the son of Amoz, which he saw concerning Judah and Jerusalem in the days of Uzziah, Jotham, Ahaz, and Hezekiah, kings of Judah …" (Isa. 1:1)—which tells us a few things about him.

ca.:
an abbreviation
of the Latin word
circa, meaning
"approximately."

- He was the son of Amoz (Isa. 1:1), about whom we know nothing else for certain. Jewish tradition suggests Amoz was the brother of Amaziah, king of Judah (ca. 798–769 BC), which would put Isaiah in the royal bloodline.

But don't quote us on that.

- He was a prophet for the southern Israelite kingdom of Judah (Isa. 1:1).

Side note: In 930 BC, after the reign of King Solomon, the nation of Israel separated into two kingdoms when northern tribes refused to accept Rehoboam (son of Solomon) as their king. The two kingdoms persisted as separate nations for the remainder of their histories, and both suffered under corrupt kings—which shouldn't have been a surprise. When God established the nation of Israel in the Promised Land, He told them that He would be their King. But they demanded an earthly one anyway. So He warned that if they established a monarchy in spite of His plan, they would suffer for their disobedience—because humans are sinful, including and especially powerful humans like the rulers who made life very difficult for the nation of Israel.

And suffer they did.

- Isaiah prophesied during the reigns of kings Uzziah (ca. 792–740 BC), Jotham (ca. 750–731 BC; Isa. 7:1), Ahaz (ca. 735–715 BC), and Hezekiah (ca. 715–686 BC).

Fun fact: the overlap of reigning dates is because sometimes a king would begin to co-reign with his father. #welovehistoryandcontext #biblenerds

More things we know:

- Isaiah was married and was a father (Isa. 7:3; 8:3, 18).
- He apparently lived in Jerusalem (Isa. 7:3 names a couple of Jerusalem locations).
- He wrote some records that are not part of Scripture (2 Chron. 26:22).
- A Jewish pseudepigraphical work dating back to first century BC reports that Isaiah was killed by being sawed in two at the order of Manasseh, king of Judah (*Martyrdom of Isaiah* 5:1–14; Heb. 11:37); the first-century work *The Lives of the Prophets* (1:1) and the Jewish Talmud (*Yevamot* 49b) refer to this as well.

Pseudepigraphical: writings that aren't in the Bible but claim to be biblical in nature.

So … that's horrific.

- The book of Isaiah is actually a collection of Isaiah's sermons and visions, given over the decades he was in ministry, between 740–680 BC.

And here's the point: Isaiah spent the better part of his life warning a rebellious, faithless generation of people to turn back to the God who loved them—which should sound familiar, because despite the almost three thousand years that have passed since Isaiah preached to the nation of Israel, like them, we have an unfortunate propensity to choose sin over God and His plan for our lives.

Gentile:
not Jewish.

But thankfully, Isaiah didn't just point out the problem. He also pointed to the One through whom Jews and Gentiles alike would (1) be reconciled to God, and (2) be made faithful.

Your Turn

5. In what ways is your pattern of behavior like that of the Old Testament nation of Israel?

6. Isaiah was tasked by God to be a mouthpiece of truth at a time when the people didn't really want to hear it. In what ways are you like Isaiah? In what ways are you not?

7. What thoughts and feelings does the phrase "God's plan" evoke in you?

Jesus Is

The first thirty-nine chapters in the book of Isaiah deal mainly with scathing condemnation and woe for Israel's tremendous sin and hardness of heart, and the resulting consequences they faced. But then it takes a turn, because after making a powerful case against God's chosen people, Isaiah began to speak words of comfort.

> Comfort, comfort my people, says your God.
> Speak tenderly to Jerusalem,
>   and cry to her
> that her warfare is ended,
>   that her iniquity is pardoned,
> that she has received from the LORD's hand
>   double for all her sins.

> A voice cries:
> "In the wilderness prepare the way of the LORD;
>   make straight in the desert a highway for our God.
> Every valley shall be lifted up,
>   and every mountain and hill be made low;
> the uneven ground shall become level,
>   and the rough places a plain.

And the glory of the LORD shall be revealed,

    and all flesh shall see it together,

    for the mouth of the LORD has spoken." (Isa. 40:1–5)

Through Isaiah, God spoke words of love over Israel during a time of their rebellion—during a time of idol worship, wandering hearts, and intense callousness to sin, not to mention all the painful consequences they were experiencing as a result of their choices. He delivered God's message of hope before their repentance.

And just so we're all on the same page, the "voice in the wilderness" that Isaiah spoke of hundreds of years before turned out to be NT John the Baptist. Like Isaiah, John preached a message of repentance but also of hope, since he told anyone who had ears to hear that the Messiah—the Savior of the world—was coming (Matt. 3).

Enter Jesus.

Jesus is the hope spoken of in the Old Testament (the Messiah) and revealed in all His glory in the New Testament—the One through whom we all have hope. Hope that our sin cycle can be broken. Hope that this world, with all its disappointment and heartache, isn't all there is. Hope that our relationship with God can be restored—and can thrive. Hope that as we follow Jesus, He'll change us from the inside out, making us joy-filled, faith-filled, and faithful.

Jesus is the **whole** point of the **whole** of Scripture—because mankind needs saving and He's it. But how does that salvation work itself out in our lives? Well, that's what we'll be covering in the coming weeks, because like those who have gone before us, **in Jesus** we find our true identity, purpose, and hope.

Your Turn

8. What do you think of Jesus? Was He a good man? A teacher of nice and pleasant things? Or something more? What is your opinion of Jesus based on?

9. Make a list of what the Bible says about Jesus in Hebrews 1:1–3:

> Long ago, at many times and in many ways, God spoke to our fathers by the prophets, but in these last days he has spoken to us by his Son, whom he appointed the heir of all things, through whom also he created the world. He is the radiance of the glory of God and the exact imprint of his nature, and he upholds the universe by the word of his power.

10. To what degree are you prepared to have your view of Jesus challenged? Are you willing to *adjust* your view of (or your response to) Him as a result?

Prayer Focus

Thank God for His intimate involvement in the lives of the people we read about in Scripture, and that He desires to be intimately involved in your life as well. **Thank** Him for choosing to communicate with you through the Bible. **Thank** Him for sending His Son, Jesus. **Ask** for His help both to understand His Word and to know Jesus more.

Further Study

Here are a few suggestions for investigating some additional connections between OT Isaiah and the NT life of Jesus.

- In Luke 2:22–35, Mary and Joseph brought the infant Jesus to the Jerusalem temple. There they met a man named Simeon, who spoke a word of praise over Jesus (2:29–32) using words from Isaiah 49:6, which means God declared things through prophets like Isaiah *before* they happened so we wouldn't miss them when they happened.

I am the LORD; I have called you in righteousness;
   I will take you by the hand and keep you;
I will give you as a covenant for the people,
   a light for the nations,
   to open the eyes that are blind,
to bring out the prisoners from the dungeon,
   from the prison those who sit in darkness.
I am the LORD; that is my name;
   my glory I give to no other,
   nor my praise to carved idols.
Behold, the former things have come to pass,
   and new things I now declare;

before they spring forth

I tell you of them. (Isa. 42:6–9)

- Luke 4:16–21 recounts one of Jesus's earliest sermons when He selected Isaiah 61:1–2 as His main text—a passage in which Isaiah prophesied about the coming Messiah. After reading, Jesus sat down and declared to the room full of people, "Today this scripture has been fulfilled in your hearing."

In other words, "The long-foretold Messiah you've been preaching about in your synagogues for centuries? I'm Him."

Needless to say, hearing a man they'd grown up with claim to be the Savior of the world didn't go over too well (Luke 4:22–30).

- Luke 7:18–23 describes a time when John the Baptist sent messengers to Jesus because he was experiencing doubt that Jesus was actually the Messiah. Instead of answering with a simple "Tell John that I AM indeed the Messiah," Jesus said:

Go and tell John what you have seen and heard: the blind receive their sight, the lame walk, lepers are cleansed, and the deaf hear, the dead are raised up, the poor have good news preached to them. (Luke 7:22)

Jesus's actions proved His identity—actions that had been described in Isaiah 29:18; 35:5–6; 42:18; and 61:1, just to name a few. Jesus asked John to draw the proper conclusion about His identity based on the physical evidence of fulfilled scripture.

"But now thus says
the LORD, he who
created you, O Jacob,
he who formed you,
O Israel: 'Fear not, for
I have redeemed you;
I have called you by
name, you are mine.'"

Isaiah 43:1

Lesson 1

What Does It Mean to Be Chosen?

YOU ARE CALLED

OMAR: Why can't you sleep?

MARY: I'm scared.

OMAR: Of what?

MARY: I don't know.

OMAR *(giving Mary a big squeeze)*: Hey. What do we do when we are scared?

MARY: We say The Words.

OMAR: Adonai's Words. From the prophet …

MARY: Isaiah.

OMAR: From the prophet Isaiah, right. "Thus says the Lord who created you, O Jacob, and He who formed you, O Israel: Fear not …" Come now, I want to hear you say it. I want to hear your pretty voice. Come.

MARY: "Fear not, for I have redeemed you; I have called you by name, you are Mine."

OMAR: "You are Mine." That's right.

Redeem: to purchase back; to ransom; to deliver from chains; to rescue and restore.

Fear Not

Fear can be like a blob monster—always on the move, always taking ground—because the list of things we fear is long. We fear loss. We fear failure. We fear not being loved. We fear disease. We fear loneliness, darkness, neediness, natural disasters, and bad guys—the list goes on into oblivion.

"I Have Called You by Name" is a fitting title for season 1, episode 1 of the *The Chosen* because no other declaration, no other truth in this world, has the power to vaporize fear like knowing and being known by God.

Why is that?

Well, truth be told, we're simple creatures in that we were made to be in relationship with God. We're designed to commune, to know and be known by our Creator, to interact with the world alongside Him and under His care. Without Him, we're at the mercy of the world around us and all the fear it brings. Without Him, there's a significant and unfillable void in our souls, because contrary to the popular self-empowerment dogma of the day, on our own we are *not* enough.

But that's okay; that's the way it's supposed to be. We're incomplete by design so that nothing but knowing and communing with God will fulfill us—not really, not permanently or completely. We're incomplete so we'll come running when the One to whom we belong calls.

Your Turn

1. What do you fear, and why? How does Psalm 139:13–18 speak to your fear?

OT Context

The prophet Isaiah experienced fear too—and who could blame him?

> In the year that King Uzziah died I saw the Lord sitting upon a throne, high and lifted up; and the train of his robe filled the temple. Above him stood the seraphim. Each had six wings; with two he covered his face, and with two he covered his feet, and with two he flew. And one called to another and said:
>
> "Holy, holy, holy is the LORD of hosts;
> the whole earth is full of his glory!"
>
> And the foundations of the thresholds shook at the voice of him who called, and the house was filled with smoke. And I said: "Woe is me! For I am lost; for I am a man of unclean lips, and I dwell in the midst of a people of unclean lips; for my eyes have seen the King, the LORD of hosts!" (Isa. 6:1–5)

Isaiah was doing whatever normal thing he was doing, when all at once, he was in the presence of the King of the Universe, along with angelic figures who were chanting praise in earth-shattering voices—and Isaiah hit the proverbial deck because not only was the experience terrifying to the senses in every possible way, it also made him acutely aware of his own moral failings. God is holy, and Isaiah felt despairingly unworthy in His presence. But at the same time, Isaiah's repentant heart was acknowledged, forgiveness was extended, and Isaiah got off the proverbial floor (Isa. 6:6–8). Or maybe he got off the actual floor.

He responded by saying yes to God's call.

And here's the takeaway: Isaiah wasn't called by God because he was worthy. He wasn't and he knew it. Moreover, God warned Isaiah that the message he would preach to the nation of Israel would fall on "deaf," unresponsive ears (Isa. 6:9–13)—but that God would persist, speaking love over His chosen people and declaring them His own before they agreed to be. In other words, Isaiah was sent to the nation of Israel while they were still sinning toward, rebelling against, and rejecting God. Which means God's message was delivered by unworthy Isaiah to unworthy people of God's own choosing.

Are you sensing a theme?

Your Turn

2. Reread Isaiah 6:3 and jot down the meanings of "holy," "Lord," and "glory." What do these words say about the One who calls us to Himself?

3. How do those words impact the way you view God? How does being in relationship with the One whom those words describe impact the things you fear?

4. Israel continued to rebel against God even as He continued calling them into relationship. What does that suggest about His character?

Worthy, Not Worthy

The notion of being called into relationship with God can bring with it some intrinsic hang-ups, like pride and insecurity that, as it turns out, are two sides of the same bad-theology coin.

Heads. Prideful people tend to see themselves as being **already worthy of God's love and approval.** By their own system of measurement, they are "good" and deserving of the corresponding spiritual status. But having an over-inflated view of ourselves can keep us from repenting and responding to God's call with our whole hearts.

Tails. Insecure people struggle to believe God's love is big enough to wipe out their personal history of wrongdoing, causing them to **feel hopelessly unworthy** of His offer to redeem and restore. But having an under-inflated view of ourselves can keep us from accepting and responding to God's call with our whole hearts.

In either case, **the focus is on us instead of God.**

Truth be told, most of us vacillate between pride and insecurity—between feeling worthy already and hopelessly unworthy—depending on the day. But take heart. Just as it was for Isaiah and the nation of Israel, God's call on our lives has very little to do with us and everything to do with Him.

Same thing was true for the people Jesus called.

Mary Magdalene was called out of the most obvious kind of darkness. Being possessed by seven demons is like the plot line of a horror movie, which means Mary didn't earn the Savior's help with good behavior. Like OT Israel, the call on her life was by divine initiative and executed by Jesus *in spite* of who she was and for the sake of who He created her to be.

Nicodemus, on the other hand, was pretty confident of his spiritual status. He was a Pharisee, set apart for the Lord's service and therefore considered by those around him to be worthy of the deference, respect, and privilege that came with his position. He likely believed he was worthy of God's calling already, which means his position and pride made him slow to see his own desperate need for reconciliation with God.

Matthew was likely too busy living for himself to care whether or not he was worthy. He was pursuing his own thing, mainly money. Regarding our coin illustration, he would've missed the lesson entirely and probably would've tossed the silver into his money bag instead! For a time, it seemed he was oblivious—or at least indifferent—to God's call on his life.

Simon wore his messy heart on his sleeve—his sometimes prideful, sometimes insecure heart on his rolled-up, gotta-earn-my-own-worth sleeve. His self-sufficiency would have been useful on a fishing boat, but it often delayed his understanding and the corresponding action when it came to following Jesus.

Incidentally, in episode 1 of *The Chosen*, Mary Magdalene serves as the ideal respondent to God's call through Jesus. Nicodemus would've been horrified by the notion: *A demonized woman from the red quarter is the model we're supposed to follow?* Matthew would've been bewildered: *What's all the fuss about? And can it be taxed?* Simon would've perhaps felt cheated: *How could she receive God's calling when I'm clearly trying harder?!*

But Mary, desperate Mary, was so hopeless that while being rescued was entirely outside the scope of her imagination, she responded at once. And with her whole heart.

To whatever degree we're prideful, insecure, or just plain desperate, God's calling happens when we aren't even aware we're broken versions of ourselves. Calling happens before God begins His transformative work of redemption, because He sees past our *before* to the *after* that He purposed and planned from the beginning. Just as He did with the nation of Israel, He sees past our fear, past our messy hearts and lives, to the people He created and loves enough to call His own.

We're valuable to God because He made us and loves us. We're valuable because He says we are, and His Word is the be-all-end-all. But He calls us to Himself because of who He is, not because we're worthy—which actually means we can be confident in our calling since it's based on His goodness, His forgiveness, and His grace (just to name a few).

Your Turn

5. Which of the four flawed-but-still-called characters in *The Chosen* do you identify with most? Do you feel worthy of being called by Jesus? Why, or why not?

6. What would you say to someone who feels unworthy of Jesus's love and call to follow Him (like Mary Magdalene)? What would you say to someone who is confident in their own goodness or self-sufficiency (like Nicodemus)?

7. Read Romans 3:10–12. Regardless of how we view our own performance record, how does the Bible say we all compare to a holy God?

Jesus Is Our Rescuer

God made the world and He loves what He made. But we humans—from the Old to the New to right now—have chosen to do our own thing, to go our own way, and to defy the laws of God's creation, the boundaries He put in place that were meant for our good and His glory. Through sin, we've separated ourselves from the One who loves us. But *because* of His love, God made a way (1) for sin to be atoned for and its power in our lives defeated, and (2) for us to know our Creator the way He intended.

> For God so loved the world, that he gave his only Son, that whoever believes in him should not perish but have eternal life. For God did not send his Son into the world to condemn the world, but in order that the world might be saved through him. Whoever believes in him is not condemned, but whoever does not believe is condemned already, because he has not believed in the name of the only Son of God. (John 3:16–18)

Jesus came to live among us; only He didn't sin. He came to rescue us from the penalty of sin, which is death and eternal separation from a holy God. He came to rescue us from sin's power over us and its daily stranglehold on our lives. And all we have to do to be forgiven and welcomed into communion with God is to believe in the One He sent.

That's it.

But also, that's everything.

None of us is worthy of God's loving attention. To be called by Him and to accept His invitation through Jesus—to be chosen and rescued in spite of our absolute unworthiness—requires us to trust Him, which includes letting Him make whatever changes to our lives He deems best. And when we do, fear no longer has a place.

Fear not, God can redeem your choices and use them for good.

Fear not, God can heal your heart, your body, and your relationships.

Fear not, you were made for more than what you've experienced so far.

Fear not, the King of the Universe has called you by name.

(Lilith stumbles into the alleyway where she takes a quick swig. She looks back to see Jesus following her onto the street.)

LILITH: Leave me alone!

(Jesus stops. Then, with all authority—)

JESUS: Mary! *(She freezes.)* Mary of Magdala!

(Mary cannot speak. Her cup falls; clay and drink crash on the ground. She slowly turns to face Him.)

MARY: Who are You? How do You know my name?

JESUS *(walking toward her as He speaks)*: Thus says the Lord who created you … and He who formed you: fear not, for I have redeemed you. I have called you by name. You are Mine.

Trinity:
the state of being three.

"God is a Trinity, Father, Son, and Holy Spirit, each an uncreated person, one in essence, equal in power and glory" (Evangelical Theological Society).

Common analogies include an egg, which has three distinct parts (shell, white, yolk) but remains one egg, or an apple, which has three distinct parts (skin, flesh, core) but remains one apple.

Of course, all analogies eventually break down, and God is not an egg or an apple. Duh.

Each member of the Trinity is not a "part" of God; each is fully God. So while we can define the word in the best possible human terms, the Trinity is a concept we won't fully understand until we're in heaven.

Your Turn

8. What do you need to be rescued from?

- A difficult personal history and pain? Mary lost her family, her dignity, and her self-control; Matthew was shunned by his family and by everyone else.
- Financial hardship? Simon and Andrew felt the weight of Roman taxation and the struggle to provide.
- A worldview that says we must save ourselves? Many Pharisees were legalistic, constantly trying to impress God and one another; Simon often took matters into his own hands, relying on his own ability, wisdom, and strength.
- Darkness, addiction, or some other sin cycle? Demons plagued Mary, causing her to feel hopeless and chained to a sinful life; Matthew was ruled by his love of money and desire for security.

9. How might Isaiah 43:1 challenge you to think differently about your situation? And what might it be calling you to do differently?

10. What does Ephesians 2:8–10 say about God's rescue of people through Jesus?

Prayer Focus

Thank God for knowing you and for wanting to be in relationship with you. **Confess** your unworthiness to be called at all. If need be, confess any pride or ego-motivated attempts to become worthy of His love through your own effort. **Praise** God for calling you to Himself in spite of all the ways you get it wrong, and for sending Jesus to rescue you and to secure your calling.

Further Study

- Read the warning about not obeying God's law in Deuteronomy 27:26 (OT), and then read where the apostle Paul quoted Deuteronomy but also provided hope in Galatians 3:10–13 (NT). Although we're cursed by an inability to obey God's laws perfectly, perfect atonement and rescue have been provided through Jesus. Take particular notice of verse 13:

  Christ redeemed us from the curse of the law by becoming a curse for us.

- Notice too that in Galatians 3:14, Paul referenced God's promised blessings to the Israelite descendants of Abraham and the plan to expand those blessings to the whole world. Check out the promise in Genesis 12:1–3 to see, once again, that the rescue plan God initiated in the Old Testament was completed through Jesus in the New Testament.
- Titus 3:4–7 addresses God's unmerited rescue of believers. Take special notice of the changes that following Jesus brings to our lives.

"When you pass
through the waters,
I will be with you;
and through the
rivers, they shall
not overwhelm you;
when you walk
through fire you
shall not be burned,
and the flame shall
not consume you."

Isaiah 43:2

Lesson 2

What Does It Mean to Be Chosen?

YOU REST

JESUS: Hello, Mary.

MARY: Hello.

(A pause.)

JESUS: It's good to see you.

MARY: Yes. Yes.

(Another pause. Jesus chuckles.)

JESUS: I don't want to be rude … but would it be okay if I—

MARY: Oh, yes, of course, please come in.

(As they approach the table …)

MARY (CONT'D): I just never thought You'd, um … I have guests here, this is my first time, I don't know what I'm doing …

JAMES/THADDEUS: Rabbi.

(Jesus nods and smiles.)

MARY: You already know these men?

JESUS: They are students of Mine. I trust they have been polite.

MARY: Of course.

(Yet another pause.)

SHULA: Your guest can take the seat, yes, Mary?

MARY: Oh, of course! Yes, of course, please have a seat. I keep saying "of course" a lot. Um, friends, this is the man I told you about, who, um, helped me.

SHULA: Oh, yes. Mary has told us so much about You.

(Mary gives her a look.)

JESUS *(smiling)*: I hope not too much.

BARNABY: I'm Barnaby. This is Shula. She's blind.

JESUS: Ah.

SHULA: In case You couldn't tell.

MARY: I'm sorry, I don't actually know Your name.

JESUS: I'm Jesus. Of Nazareth.

BARNABY: Well, apparently something good *can* come from Nazareth!

(No one laughs. Mary glares at him. Jesus chuckles, winks at Barnaby.)

JESUS: Mary, I'm honored to be here. Why don't you begin.

MARY: Oh, no, I couldn't. Now that You're here, You must.

JESUS: Thank you, but this is your home, and I would love for you to do it.

(Mary pulls out her paper. Takes a deep breath.)

MARY: Okay. I'll just, uh, read from this now?

(Jesus nods and smiles.)

MARY (CONT'D):

"Now the heavens and the earth were completed and all their host …

And God completed on the seventh day His work that He did, and God abstained on the seventh day from all His work He did.

And God blessed the seventh day and He hallowed it, for thereon He abstained from all the work that God created to do …"

Shabbat

Typically we equate sleep with rest. While our eyes are open, we go a hundred miles an hour, often measuring the value of our days by how much we can accomplish. Good days are busy ones full of going, seeing, doing, exploring, conquering, and completing. And then at night, when we're no longer physically capable of doing all the things, we stop for a moment to "rest."

"Shabbat" is the title of season 1, episode 2 of *The Chosen* and the Hebrew translation of the word *Sabbath*, which means to cease from work, because as the fourth commandment states:

Shabbat: pronounced shuh-baat.

> Remember the Sabbath day, to keep it holy. Six days you shall labor, and do all your work, but the seventh day is a Sabbath to the LORD your God. On it you shall not do any work, you, or your son, or your daughter, your male servant, or your female servant, or your livestock, or the sojourner who is within your gates. For in six days the LORD made heaven and earth, the sea, and all that is in them, and rested on the seventh day. Therefore the LORD blessed the Sabbath day and made it holy. (Ex. 20:8–11)

So the Sabbath was and is a day of communal observance that God's people do together, primarily marked by abstinence from work—though that's not all it's about. Having a day off each week is a perk, for sure, and God built it into His system because He's gracious to His creation and intimately in tune with our needs. We *need* a day off to hit the reset button, to attend church, and to spend time with people we love—because of course we do. But none of that compares to God's primary intention behind the commandment.

Stick a pin in that.

Your Turn

1. Reread Exodus 20:8–11. What is the origin of Sabbath-day rest?

OT Context

When God rescued the Israelites from slavery in Egypt, He guided them *into* the wilderness under the leadership of Moses. But the miracles-via-plagues that convinced Pharaoh to eventually release the Jews made it clear that God was the One in charge. As the story goes, Pharaoh soon changed his mind, and he chased them to the edge of the Red Sea, where God opened the waters allowing the Israelites to cross on dry land. When Pharaoh and his army pursued, God released the waters, crushing the entire Egyptian army and ensuring Israel's future freedom (Ex. 14:10–30).

But then came the wilderness on the other side. God told the Israelites they would be led to a promised land "flowing with milk and honey," but they didn't know the way or how far a walk it was. Instead, all they saw were the impossible things in front of them—the heat, the dust, the distance. No shade, no food supply, little water. And then there were the impossible things on the *other* side of the wilderness—land already conquered and inhabited—which meant more kings, more armies, and more impossible things.

Standing at the edge of the wilderness, they couldn't have known that God Himself would guide their steps: "And the LORD went before them by day in a pillar of cloud to lead them along the way, and by night in a pillar of fire to give them light, that they might travel by day and by night. The pillar of cloud by day and the pillar of fire by night did not depart from before the people" (Ex. 13:21–22).

They couldn't have known that God would provide "bread from heaven" (Ex. 16:4)—a daily collection of manna for their food, including a double portion on the sixth day so they could obey His command to rest on the seventh: "'See! The LORD has given you the Sabbath; therefore on the sixth day he gives you bread for two days. Remain each of you in his place; let no one go out of his place on the seventh day.' So the people rested on the seventh day" (Ex. 16:29–30).

They couldn't have known that God would keep their sandals and clothing from ever wearing out (Deut. 29:5) or that He would deliver kings and kingdoms into their hands without requiring them to lift a sword.

They couldn't have known what they quickly came to know:

That God's provision—including rest—is an overflow of His presence.

Manna was "bread from heaven," but that doesn't mean it literally fell from the sky like rain. It seems to have materialized like dew, which is how it's described in Exodus 16:13–14: "a thin flaky substance that appeared on the ground.

Later in the chapter, it's compared to coriander seed and described as "white, and it tasted like wafers with honey" (16:31).

Your Turn

2. What promise did God make to His chosen people in Isaiah 43:2?

3. How does the wording of this verse relate to Exodus 14:26–31? Joshua 3:14–17? Daniel 3:1–28?

4. The One who made the wilderness was the One leading the Israelites through it. How does meditating on God as the Creator change the way you look at impossible things?

Wellspring of Rest

The Jews of first-century Israel weren't much better off than their wilderness-wandering ancestors. They were living in their own country but under oppressive Roman occupation and rule. Their continued observance of the Sabbath served as a reminder that God had always been faithful to provide for the needs of His chosen people, but they still longed for relief from their circumstances.

Yet according to Isaiah 43:2, relief and rest don't necessarily come from circumstances being removed. Rather, they come from God's presence, no matter the circumstance.

"When you pass through the waters, I will be with you …"

Mary Magdalene experienced Jesus's rescuing power in her life. But being freed from her demons didn't automatically remove her difficult circumstances. No doubt she still had painful memories, relationships that were strained or broken, and consequences that came from life gone awry. But also, she had Jesus.

No wonder she ended up becoming one of His devoted followers, exchanging the roof over her head for a tent, and familiarity for a whole new kind of wilderness wandering. She had found the kind of rest that only comes from communing with the Creator, and she wasn't about to lose His presence.

Nicodemus had built a decent life for himself. But while good behavior, success, and money have the power to make life easier, they don't satisfy the soul. Neither does a works-based religion. Adherence to the Sabbath as God commanded was a good thing, but only if it resulted in gratefulness for and worship of the Creator. While Nicodemus's *Shabbat* gatherings would've been the most ritually respectful—no doubt there was significant emphasis placed on proper observance of OT law—rituals have the potential to distract from proper observance of God's presence.

Matthew had found a way to benefit from the Roman occupation, and as a result, he likely wasn't invited to many *Shabbat* dinners. Relational fallout would've been unavoidable, though perhaps for a time he was able to ignore the loneliness that came with the tax-man territory. But striving after personal gain leads us away from our Creator—away from any hope we have of experiencing true rest and peace.

Simon might've been among those most ready for God to intervene in Israel's difficult circumstances. Overwhelmed by financial hardship, he likely struggled with impatience—maybe even his faith. Perhaps he wondered when God would relieve Israel's suffering and restore their freedom. Perhaps he wondered if God still cared about His chosen people at all—wonderings that would've made *Shabbat* remembrances painful and confusing.

In any case, Mary is again the example we should aspire to follow. She wasn't striving to obey a commandment in order to earn God's favor; she knew she'd already received His gracious and unmerited favor. Instead, she was eager to set aside time to remember her Creator, the One who knew her by name—to enter into His presence and celebrate what He'd done and what He would do. Compared to Nicodemus's *Shabbat* dinner, Mary's was humble and imperfect, but far more glorious.

And it didn't hurt that Jesus was in the room.

Your Turn

5. When it comes to practicing your own Sabbath-day rest, which character do you relate to the most, and why?

6. Psalm 46:10 says, "Be still, and know that I am God." How would meditating on God have impacted Mary's healing process? Nicodemus's priorities? Matthew's striving? Simon's impatience or confusion?

7. Keeping the Sabbath is most obviously marked by not working. But God's primary intention behind the commandment is to spend the day like Mary did—to enter into His presence. What needs to change in your schedule or in your mind-set to rest the way God intended?

Jesus Is Present

The Sabbath celebrates God's miraculous rescue of His people from Egypt, His daily provision for them in the wilderness, and Israel's total dependence on Him. But remembering God's faithfulness to the chosen people of the OT isn't the endgame; it serves as our reminder that He remains faithful. That He's present right now. That He's still providing, leading, and working on behalf of His chosen people. And that He's worthy of *our* ongoing dependence.

> "[Jesus said,] 'Come to me, all who labor and are heavy laden, and I will give you rest. Take my yoke upon you, and learn from me, for I am gentle and lowly in heart, and you will find rest for your souls. For my yoke is easy, and my burden is light.'"
>
> Matthew 11:28–30

Jesus doesn't instruct weary, burdened people to sleep more, caffeinate more, or take a vacation. Instead, He invites us to come to Him, and when we do, He provides us with rest. While we can rest our bodies anytime we choose, *soul rest* only happens in the presence of our Creator. The One who knows the number of hairs on our heads (Matt. 10:30; Luke 12:7) and keeps track of our sorrows (Ps. 56:8). The One intimately aware of our unique challenges and all the ways He's going to use them for good (Rom. 8:28). The One who loves us enough to be our rescuer—in spite of our sin and struggle—knowing what it would cost Him (Rom. 5:8). And the One leading us through water and flame to the Promised Land of heaven, where there will be no more fear, pain, or strife (Rev. 21:4).

In His presence, we experience provision and peace and rest that supersede hard things—because of who He is.

MARY (CONT'D):

"Now the heavens and the earth were completed and all their host …

And God completed on the seventh day His work that He did, and God abstained on the seventh day from all His work He did.

And God blessed the seventh day and He hallowed it, for thereon He abstained from all His work that God created to do.

Blessed are You, Lord our God, Ruler of the Universe, who creates the fruit of the vine …

You have lovingly and willingly given us Your *Shabbat* as an inheritance in memory of creation …

Because it is the first day of our holy assemblies, in memory of the exodus from Egypt.

Blessed are You, Lord, our God, King of the Universe, who brings forth bread from the earth.

Amen."

Your Turn

8. Jesus's promise in Matthew 11:28–30 is reminiscent of the promise in Isaiah 43:2, in that Jesus doesn't say there will be no responsibilities or hardship ("yoke" or "burden"). Instead, He stays with us and provides a way through. How does knowing that impact the way you feel about or respond to your circumstances?

9. Fill in the blank: God is with me in _____.

10. Reread Psalm 56:8; Matthew 10:30; Luke 12:7; Romans 5:8; 8:28; and Revelation 21:4. Which of these verses bring you feelings of rest, peace, and hope? Why?

Prayer Focus

Give thanks to God for the soul rest He offers through Jesus. Give thanks to Him for daily provisions like food, clothes, shelter, and friends. **Thank** Him that His presence allows you to endure and overcome hard circumstances this side of eternity. **Ask** Jesus to teach you more and more how to rest in His presence. **Tell** Him how excited you are for the perfect and pain-free rest that awaits us in heaven.

Further Study

- Read 1 Samuel 15:10–23; Isaiah 1:9–20; Jeremiah 7:21–28; and Amos 4:1–13. These passages indicate that God was displeased with people who kept Sabbath-like celebrations for the wrong reasons—even comparing His chosen people to godless pagans persisting in unrepentant sin while giving the appearance of religious dedication.

  Yikes.

- Read Isaiah 56:1–8. The Sabbath was not designed as a means for getting God's attention or as a way to earn His approval. Rather, it was a means for the people of God to remember His creation of them and to demonstrate their dependence on Him. Isaiah noted that the invitation to this kind of faith dependence—a dependence expressed by keeping the Sabbath—was not just for the OT Israelite nation, but for all who would put their trust in the Lord.

- Read Acts 20:7; 1 Corinthians 16:1–2; Matthew 28:1–10; Mark 16:1–8; Luke 24:1–12; and John 20:1–19. Saturday, the seventh day of the week and the Jewish day of worship practiced by Jesus and His followers, is still the day of worship for Judaism and for a few branches of Christianity. Yet most Christians set aside Sunday, the first day of the week, as the primary day to rest from work and gather for corporate worship.

Which means something very significant must've happened in order to get a bunch of religiously concerned Jews to change how they observed one of the ten most important commandments in their whole belief system. #resurrectionsunday

Betcha didn't know that by worshipping together on Sundays, Christians celebrate Easter every week. #heisrisenindeed

"For I am the LORD your God, the Holy One of Israel, your Savior. I give Egypt as your ransom, Cush and Seba in exchange for you. Because you are precious in my eyes, and honored, and I love you, I give men in return for you, peoples in exchange for your life."

Isaiah 43:3–4

Lesson 3

What Does It Mean to Be Chosen?

YOU ARE CHERISHED

CHILD #4: Where were You yesterday?

JESUS: I had to stay in town later on; there was a woman who needed my help.

CHILD #3: Did You build something for her?

JESUS: No … do you remember when I said that I have a job that is bigger than My trade? There is a woman who has had much pain in her life, and she was in trouble, so I helped her.

JOSHUA: Is she Your friend?

JESUS: She is now. And I have chosen her and others, and more soon, to join Me in traveling.

ABIGAIL: Do they know You?

JESUS: Not yet.

CHILD #1: But what if they don't like You?

JESUS (laughing): Many won't. This is My reason for being here.

ABIGAIL: I still don't understand. What is Your reason for being here?

(Jesus takes a moment. The children lean in as He talks quietly but firmly.)

JESUS: I'm telling you this because even though you are children, and the elders in your life have lived longer, many times adults need the faith of children. And if you hold on to this faith, really tightly, someday soon you will understand all of what I am saying to you.

But you ask an important question, Abigail. What is My reason for being here? And the answer is for all of you:

"The Spirit of the Lord is upon Me. He has anointed Me to proclaim good news to the poor. He has sent Me to proclaim liberty to the captives and recovering of sight to the blind, to set at liberty those who are oppressed, to proclaim the year of the Lord's favor."

JOSHUA: Isaiah.

JESUS *(nodding)*: Isaiah.

Precious in His Sight

One of the most well-known Sunday school songs of all-time was written more than one hundred years ago, but it declares a timeless truth in its lyrics: "Jesus loves the little children, all the children of the world. Red and yellow, black and white, they are precious in His sight. Jesus loves the little children of the world."

While political correctness would like to banish such notions, the song stubbornly endures because its message resonates deeply and profoundly and universally: we were made in the image of God, and God loves what He has made.

This episode of *The Chosen* is titled "Jesus Loves the Little Children," but it's not just about children. When it comes to God's love, it's not about our age, our appearance, our abilities, or anything else we may or may not bring to the table. It's about what already is.

We are precious to our Maker.

Your Turn

1. What does our sweet little song have in common with Galatians 3:28?

OT Context

In the Old Testament era, the people of God were sometimes described as the children of God (Ex. 4:22; Hos. 1:10–11; 11:1), and occasionally God was referred to as a father (Isa. 63:16; 64:8; Jer. 31:9–11) or compared to a mother (Isa. 49:13–16). Of course, the point is that God loves His chosen people the way good parents love their children. Good parents do anything, endure anything, sacrifice anything to care for their own. Now multiply that by a gazillion, and you're in the ballpark of God's love for His chosen people.

Just as a parent pursues a wayward child, time and again God pursued the nation of Israel (1) at great cost, (2) to great lengths, and (3) with unrelenting mercy and grace. According to Isaiah 43, God demonstrated just how far He would go to bring His people back, including ransoming other nations in their place (stay tuned for more on that). Naturally, the mention of Egypt brings to mind the exodus rescue. For the people of Isaiah's day, they could look back and see that God had been faithful all the way from Egypt to the Promised Land. But then His protection and provision extended further—to Cush and Seba and beyond—because God cherished His chosen people, which is why He wouldn't let them go.

Mercy:
not receiving the
punishment we deserve.

Grace:
receiving an undeserved gift.

Cush is in northeastern Africa (sometimes called "Ethiopia" back then, but not the same as today's Ethiopia!).

We're not sure where Seba was located, but it was most likely somewhere along the Red Sea.

Your Turn

2. What are some characteristics of a good parent?

3. Having a not-very-good parent can negatively affect the way we see and respond to God. Read Jeremiah 31:9–11 below and underline all the ways God is a good Father:

> With weeping they shall come,
>   and with pleas for mercy I will lead them back,
> I will make them walk by brooks of water,
>   in a straight path in which they shall not stumble,
> for I am a father to Israel,
>   and Ephraim is my firstborn.
>
> Hear the word of the LORD, O nations,
>   and declare it in the coastlands far away;
> say, "He who scattered Israel will gather him,
>   and will keep him as a shepherd keeps his flock."
> For the LORD has ransomed Jacob
>   and has redeemed him from hands too strong for him. (Jer. 31:9–11)

4. God pursued Israel, in spite of their wanton rebellion. Compare what they deserved to receive from God with what they actually received from God, time and again.

Welcomed

> "Then children were brought to [Jesus] that he might lay his hands on them and pray.
> The disciples rebuked the people, but Jesus said, 'Let the little children come to me
> and do not hinder them, for to such belongs the kingdom of heaven.'"
>
> Matthew 19:13–14

That last part would've been a head scratcher for those listening, because parents in the ancient world didn't appreciate childhood the same way we do. It's not that parents had loveless, utilitarian attitudes toward their children; on the contrary, children were thought of as blessings to their parents (Deut. 28:1–6; Ps. 103:13; 127:3–5; 128:3–4; Matt. 2:16–18; John 4:46–54). But in first century AD, a person's contribution heavily weighted their value, and young children couldn't contribute much. While modern Western culture has extended childhood into the early twenties—have mercy—children in ancient times were expected to start working as soon as physically possible. Childhood was simply not a cherished time of life and definitely ended at puberty, which may be the reason the Gospels say nothing about the childhood experiences of our four main characters.

And yet we can surmise based on what we do know.

Mary Magdalene was from the town of Magdala, a place known for being so morally bankrupt that Rome ultimately destroyed the city for its corruption. Whether or not Mary experienced a godly Jewish upbringing, through life's tragedies and demonic influence, she slipped into a life of debauchery. Mary likely didn't feel precious to anyone, and wickedness and evil had a stranglehold on her life.

Nicodemus, a teacher among the Pharisees, probably had a solid Jewish upbringing. Perhaps he was like another famous Pharisee in the New Testament, the apostle Paul, who remarked, "My manner of life from my youth, spent from the beginning among my own nation and in Jerusalem, is known by all the Jews ... that according to the strictest party of our religion I have lived as a Pharisee" (Acts 26:4–5).

Sounds like a real hoot. In any event, it's likely Nicodemus felt pride over his heritage, accomplishments, and stature rather than feeling cherished by God for who he was.

Matthew also likely benefited from a childhood with godly training and education; his historic Hebrew name, Levi, indicates as much. But that didn't stop him from choosing to serve Rome. Like other Jews who willingly worked for the enemy, Matthew got rich by betraying his fellow citizens. His family would've been damaged by his open display of disloyalty.

By pursuing the promise of wealth, Matthew willingly gave up any sense of being cherished for who he was. Contrary to the meaning of his name ("gift of God"), Matthew chose instead to be paid for what he could do.

Simon was a man of meager learning (Acts 4:13), but staying faithful to the God of his fathers was instilled in him from his youth. Nicodemus's pride in being religiously accomplished was not available to Simon, nor was Matthew's financial self-sufficiency—such things were beyond Simon Peter's reach. But from what we do know of the fisherman-turned-follower, he was the kind of guy who suffered from *both* pride and self-sufficiency and perhaps would've been entirely uncomfortable with the sentimental notion of being cherished.

Abigail and Joshua are fictional children created for *The Chosen*, but they're based on actual interactions, as well as Jesus's words *about* children: *to such belongs the kingdom of heaven.* Unlike most of the adults who came in contact with Jesus, the children knew they had nothing of value to offer Him except their love and excitement to be there—and Jesus welcomed them. He wanted to spend time with them, hug them, and heal them. He *wanted* to. He accepted them, not because of who they were or what they could do, but because of who He is and what He does.

Your Turn

5. According to Matthew 18:1–4, what quality do children have that we should seek to emulate?

6. Whose imagined childhood experience do you most identify with? Mary's darkness and brokenness? Nicodemus's need to perform and earn his worth? Matthew's rebellion and isolation? Simon's constant struggle to make a life for himself?

7. Read each of their actual come-to-Jesus stories in Luke 8:1–3; John 3:1–12; Matthew 9:9–13; and Luke 5:1–11. In spite of having vastly different life experiences, what do all four of these people have in common? (Hint, hint: the thing they have in common with each other is the same thing they actually have in common with children.)

Jesus Is Our Keeper

It's easy to understand why children are welcomed and cherished by Jesus. Children are uncomplicated. They're appropriately awestruck by the world around them. They're cute and innocent and vulnerable and unvarnished. They're wide-eyed, expectant, moldable, and trusting—unlike us. They're not jaded or judgmental, self-reliant, self-promoting, or stained by a lifetime of sinful choices, which means it's much harder to believe we're cherished by God the way they are. That we could be the recipients of His perfect love.

But that's exactly what we are, and the evidence can be traced all the way back to Isaiah: "I give men in return for you, peoples in exchange for your life" (Isa. 43:4).

Ransoms are paid to keep what would otherwise be lost. As indicated by Isaiah some seven centuries before Jesus arrived, God

Ransom: a sum of money or other payment demanded or paid for the return of a prisoner.

cherishes His chosen people so much that He ransoms them back for Himself. He keeps them, no matter the cost.

> "You were ransomed from the futile ways inherited from your forefathers,
>
> not with perishable things such as silver or gold, but with the precious
>
> blood of Christ, like that of a lamb without blemish or spot."
>
> 1 Peter 1:18–19

When sin was stealing us away, Jesus became our ransom. He came in service of us, to exchange His life for ours, to be the "ransom for many" (Mark 10:45) and to return to God His chosen people "from every tribe and language and people and nation" (Rev. 5:9). We are clearly cherished by our Maker—in spite of having nothing to give—because He pursues and forgives and redeems and keeps.

JESUS: I have loved spending this time with you. You are all so very special. And I hope that My next students ask the same questions you do and that they listen to My answers. But I suspect they do not have the understanding you do.
(He looks at Abigail.)
And I hope that when the time comes, they will tell others about Me like you have.
CAMPSITE (NIGHT)
(Jesus puts the finishing touches on something we don't see, and He sets it down next to a rock. We then see Him writing something with coal on the rock. He smiles, and we—CUT TO:)
FIELD (MORNING)
(Abigail is walking alone with her doll. She rounds the corner to the campsite and freezes. We see the site is empty. Other than a lifeless fire pit, everything is gone. Well, not quite everything. As Abigail approaches, we see a simple but well-crafted dollhouse: rock slabs held together by first-century rope. Abigail notices the writing above it and reads aloud.)

ABIGAIL: "Abigail, I know you can read. You are very special. This is for you. I did not come only for the wealthy."

Your Turn

8. In order to keep us, Jesus became like us. According to the apostle Paul in Philippians 2:5–8, what did that entail?

9. How should you respond to the idea that Jesus cherishes you enough to (a) ransom Himself as payment for your sin and (b) restore your relationship with God?

10. Not only did Jesus become like us to keep us, He also promises to make us more like Him—which is exactly what He did in the lives of Mary, Matthew, and Simon Peter. Read Galatians 5:18–24 and make a list of the characteristics that become ours through the power of His Holy Spirit.

Prayer Focus

Give thanks to Jesus for sacrificing Himself in your place in order to bring you back to your Maker. **Ask** God to **empower** you to have a childlike faith (not a childish faith) and to **trust** that He'll keep you through the hardships of life. You might even consider **praying** the words in Jude 1:24–25: "Now to him who is able to keep you from stumbling and to present you blameless before the presence of his glory with great joy, to the only God, our Savior, through Jesus Christ our Lord, be glory, majesty, dominion, and authority, before all time and now and forever. Amen."

Further Study

- The Old Testament encourages strong family relationships and family-based training on faith in God. For example, in the passage that inspires the daily prayer of the Jews called the *Shema* (recited by the children in episode 3), Moses reminded the Israelites of their responsibility to not only teach their children about their covenant relationship with God but to also conduct their whole lives around that relationship.

   Hear, O Israel: The LORD our God, the LORD is one. You shall love the LORD your God with all your heart and with all your soul and with all your might. And these words that I command you today shall be on your heart. You shall teach them diligently to your children, and shall talk of them when you sit in your house, and when you walk by the way, and when you lie down, and when you rise. You shall bind them as a sign on your hand, and they shall be as frontlets between your eyes. You shall write them on the doorposts of your house and on your gates. (Deut. 6:4–9)

- As we mentioned, God is addressed as "Father" in the Old Testament (Isa. 63:16; 64:8). Jesus also referred to God as "Father" but used the more intimate Aramaic word *Abba*, which is a near equivalent to the modern-day English word for "Daddy" (Mark 14:36). This way of referring to God was unprecedented in Jesus's day. As the one and only Son of God, Jesus has a unique relationship to the Father in the Trinity (John 1:14; 5:17–47; 10:22–39; 20:17); nevertheless, He encourages His followers to also address God as "Father" (Matt. 6:5–15; Luke 11:1–4) and "*Abba*" (Rom. 8:15; Gal. 4:6).

- John 17 records a conversation Jesus had with the Father just prior to His arrest and crucifixion. He clearly knew the part He would play in the plan of salvation, and that He would soon be called back to heaven, so He prayed for His followers. Notice that He asked God to keep His followers safe while He would be gone (17:11), to keep them "in [His] name" (17:12), and to not remove them from the world but to protect them from the devil (17:15). Notice too that Jesus's prayer was not only for His twelve apostles or the other first-century believers; Jesus included everyone who would become a believer through the testimonies of those first followers (17:20). Which means we are mentioned in the Bible (!) and that Jesus prayed for us (Rom. 8:34).

Mind. Blown.

"Fear not, for I am with you;
I will bring your offspring
from the east, and from
the west I will gather you.
I will say to the north, Give
up, and to the south, Do
not withhold; bring my
sons from afar and my
daughters from the end of
the earth, everyone who is
called by my name, whom
I created for my glory,
whom I formed and made."

Isaiah 43:5–7

Lesson 4

What Does It Mean to Be Chosen?

YOU CHANGE COURSE

SIMON: A few days ago, I looked you in the eyes and told you I had … "this." I lied. I'm sorry.

EDEN: What do you—

SIMON: I've been fishing on *Shabbat* because I've had no choice. Andrew's had tax debts, I've got tax debts, we haven't been able to keep up. I did some things I'm not proud of to fix it, and now it's gone bad, and we're in trouble.

EDEN: "We"? What is—

SIMON: I. I'm in trouble, but "we" because I need a miracle, or I could be in big trouble.

EDEN: Simon, I'm not a child, stop speaking in riddles. Tell me—

SIMON: I could go to prison. We could lose the house.

(She steps back.)

EDEN: What?!

SIMON: The cut on my ear … it's from a Roman, and—

EDEN: Simon!

SIMON: If I don't catch a ton of fish or get some help somehow, they'll arrest me.

EDEN: Or kill you! They're Romans!

SIMON: So I need to go now, and—

EDEN: Go where?

SIMON: To fish. I've gotta spend the rest of the week doing nothing but catch every fish I can and hope I can fix this somehow.

(She turns away in fear, disgust, everything.)

SIMON (CONT'D): So that's why we can't take in *Eema*, it's just not—

(She whips back around.)

*Eema:
the Hebrew
word for
"Mother."*

EDEN: She has nothing to do with this; I'm not going to let you punish her for your sins!

SIMON: Eden, you can't—

EDEN: You know nothing of what I can or can't do; you've had your eyes closed around here! And God is with me, even if you aren't.

SIMON: I'm sorry.

EDEN: Where is your faith?

SIMON: What?

EDEN: You heard me.

SIMON: Faith isn't going to get me more fish.

Forego Control

Most of us like being in the driver's seat. We'd rather follow the navigator on our phones than wait for someone else to tell us where to turn—because we like to look ahead. We want to see what's coming and to know exactly how many miles are between us and our destination. We want to choose the route, which lane to be in, what's playing on the radio, and whatever fast-food drive-through strikes our fancy.

We want to be in control.

Incidentally, so does God, and when we belong to Him, His way of doing things trumps ours. Or at least, that's how it's supposed to work. In episode 4 of *The Chosen* called "The Rock on Which It Is Built," Simon Peter is in the driver's seat—or whatever the fishing boat equivalency of a driver's seat is.

And it isn't going very well.

Your Turn

1. What area of your life do you find most difficult to relinquish control of (relationships, job, future plans)? What does James 4:13–15 recommend instead?

OT Context

As we've been studying, Israel was God's chosen nation—but not because Israel was awesome. On the contrary. In spite of being chosen, preserved, protected, led, loved, and set apart since the beginning of time, they repeatedly disobeyed and rejected God. Israel was chosen because their Creator wanted to display His love and sovereignty through them; they were chosen because of *His* awesomeness, not their own. But in spite of His favor, eventually the nation sinned its way into a civil war, resulting in two nations instead of one: Israel the northern kingdom and Judah the southern. Both were unfaithful in following God, although Judah managed to have a handful of kings who sort-of obeyed. With their occasionally faithful leaders, Judah occasionally reaped the rewards of obedience—God continued to bear with His people, proving His perfect faithfulness and mercy again and again.

Then along came King Ahaz, who botched things royally. (See what we did there?)

Ahaz became king of Judah around 735 BC, just a few years into Isaiah's ministry. While the four kings before him followed God, Ahaz didn't. He worshipped foreign gods, crafted idols and altars in their honor, and even burned his own son as an offering. But then Israel and Syria formed an alliance against Judah, and the gods of Ahaz offered no help or peace. "Ahaz and the heart[s] of his people shook as the trees of the forest shake before the wind" (Isa. 7:2).

And rightly so. Judah was small and, by all human accounts, vulnerable. But then God sent Isaiah to prophesy to the sinful king, telling him to **repent and return** to the one true God, and Judah would be spared (Isa. 8:11–13). But the king ignored the prophet's warning and instead trusted in what his eyes could see—and it was to his kingdom's demise. To save himself from men, Ahaz turned to men. He begged and bribed Assyria to join the fight on his behalf, and indeed they came to Judah's defense. They conquered the northern Israelites and took them captive and then forced Ahaz to serve as a vassal king in subjection to Assyria, costing him the very freedom he sought to protect.

Well done, Ahaz.

Thankfully, God's faithfulness didn't end with the king's disobedience and subsequent demise. God's promise to gather the nation of Israel back to Himself—to correct their doomed course—would be fulfilled not only by bringing the people back from Assyria and then again from Babylon; His promise to gather His chosen would ultimately be fulfilled by the coming Messiah.

Your Turn

2. Judah's foolish king wanted to maintain his sense of control, but God was already (and still is) in control of everything and everyone. Which begs the question, what do you think would've happened to Syria and Israel's conspiracy against Judah if King Ahaz had turned back to the one true King?

3. In Isaiah 43:5, God said, "Fear not, for I am with you"—which makes sense, for all the reasons we've been studying (God is our Rescuer, our Provider, our Keeper). But in Isaiah 8:11–13, who did God tell Isaiah we *should* fear?

4. Read Deuteronomy 10:20–11:7. In your own words, explain the reasons Moses gave for why Israel should serve God with reverence and fear.

I Was ... but God ... and Now

God's message for King Ahaz was the same He'd given to Israel time and again: repent and return. But most of them didn't, and so they forfeited His presence and the protection that came with it. By first century AD, Rome had taken over most of the known world, including the Promised Land. Rather than forcing them into exile, Israel was invaded and occupied, which meant that without even leaving their homeland, the Jews once again suffered under a foreign power.

It's no wonder they were desperate for a Savior—someone who would rescue them and restore their freedom, their way of life, their hope. They were looking for the prophesied Messiah and collectively assumed He would overthrow Rome and establish His kingdom, but they were wrong. Jesus didn't come to save the Jews from their political enslavement. He came to save us all from our sin enslavement.

Unfortunately, like Israel, most of us would rather be rescued from our problems than deal with our sin. But our biggest problem *is* our sin and that we choose it over God. As a result, it's actually sin that sits in the driver's seat of our lives, not us. Like the fools we are, we strap ourselves in, tell ourselves we're the ones controlling the wheel, and then blame God when we land in a ditch.

Thing is, belonging to God isn't about taking His help, provision, and protection whenever we feel like it. It's about repenting and returning to our Creator and one true King—the One who knows everything, controls everything, and works all things "together for good, for those who are called according to [God's] purpose" (Rom. 8:28). When we repent and return to Him, our lives change and we become the people He intended for us to be—just like our New Testament brothers and sisters. Because the change experienced by every follower of Jesus—whether living in the first century or the twenty-first century—can be summed up like this: I was. But God. And now.

Mary Magdalene was broken and ruled by evil, cut off, cast aside, and ashamed of who she'd become. **But God** rescued her, accepted her, and restored her. **And now** she's remembered for being among those who faithfully followed Jesus—even financially supporting His ministry—and the first person He revealed Himself to after the resurrection.

Nicodemus was self-centered, proud, and confident in his own ability to lead. **But God** humbled him and was patient with his questions, even his lack of faith. **And now** he's remembered for seeking answers from Jesus, which brought him a lot closer to actually having them.

"The thing
that happened
in between
was Him."

Matthew was rebellious, isolated, and hated for serving the enemy. **But God** pursued him anyway, called him to follow, and welcomed him into His family. **And now** he's remembered for serving Jesus, being one of the twelve apostles, and writing the first book in the New Testament.

Simon was self-sufficient, brash, and impulsive—"like a wave of the sea that is driven and tossed by the wind" (James 1:6). **But God** revealed Simon's limitations to him and called him to follow the One who has no limitations (#miracleofthefish). **And now** Simon is remembered for being faithful and steady and for living up to the name Jesus gave him: Peter, which means "Rock."

> And on this rock I will build my church, and the gates of hell shall
> not prevail against it. (Matt. 16:18)

To **repent** of our sin and **return** to our Creator requires a change of course. By definition, following Jesus means going where *He goes* and doing what *He does*, not choosing for ourselves. It means surrendering the control we think we have to Him—to climb into the passenger's seat and hand Jesus the keys. It means believing His way is better than ours. It means trusting that God will lead us as faithfully and as lovingly as He did the nation of Israel and that over time we'll become more like Jesus and less like the *was* we once were.

Your Turn

5. What's your come-to-Jesus story?
(Side note: Every stage is a process, so don't feel bad if your story is still unfolding.)

I was _____ .

But God _____ .

And now _____ .

6. Read Luke 5:1–11. The moment Simon realized he was completely unworthy to be in Jesus's presence was also the moment he left everything behind to follow Jesus and remain in His presence. Explain the correlation.

7. Following Jesus means surrendering to Him. What do the words *surrender* and (even more controversial) *submission* mean to you?

Jesus Is Our Leader

Most of us don't like submitting. In addition to our strong desire to be in control, we find the notion insulting, sometimes even degrading. But it's simply not possible to retain control and follow at the same time—and following Jesus is required to be in relationship with Him.

> And when [Jesus] had finished speaking, he said to Simon, "Put out into the deep and let down your nets for a catch." And Simon answered, "Master, we toiled all night and took nothing! But at your word I will let down the nets." And when they had done this, they enclosed a large number of fish, and their nets were breaking. They signaled to their partners in the other boat to come and help them. And they came and filled both the boats, so that they began to sink. But when Simon Peter saw it, he fell down at Jesus' knees, saying, "Depart from me, for I am a sinful man, O Lord" … And Jesus said to [him], "Do not be afraid; from now on you will be catching men." And when they had brought their boats to land, they left everything and followed him. (Luke 5:4–8, 10–11)

Leaving everything behind was quite literal for these guys; their livelihoods were 100 percent dependent on their boats and fishing gear, not to mention their time on the water. But when Simon Peter realized Jesus was the promised Messiah, he got real low, real fast.

Any previously held notion of control disappeared, and in its place were deference and a desire to serve the One who was *actually* in control. And then Simon did the only logical thing …

He surrendered and called Jesus "Lord."

Lord: someone with power and authority over another; Master, Ruler.

SIMON: My brother, and the baptizer … they … You are the Lamb of God, yes?

JESUS: I am.

SIMON: Depart from me; I'm a sinful man. You don't know who I am, the things I've done …

JESUS: Don't be afraid, Simon.

SIMON: I'm sorry, we've waited for You for so long, we believed, but my faith how sorry.

JESUS: Lift up your head, fisherman.

SIMON: What do You want from me? Anything You ask, I will do.

JESUS: Follow Me.

(Simon looks into His eyes, seeing something in them he's never seen before. And he's transfixed.)

SIMON: I will.

Your Turn

8. Explain in your own words why salvation through faith in Jesus is free but following Him costs us everything.

9. Read Matthew 7:21–23, in which Jesus clearly stated that not all people who claim to know Him actually do. What is the evidence of a true follower? (Hint, hint: reread the second half of verse 21.)

10. What area of your life do you need to leave behind in order to follow Jesus more fully?

Prayer Focus

If you've never surrendered to Jesus as Lord, **change** that today; you can even **say** the words that Simon Peter said. If you're already a Jesus follower, **thank** Him once again for dying for your sins, for raising you to new life in Him, and for patiently and faithfully leading you. **Ask** Him to give you specific direction for the decisions you have to make and for the way you need to go. **Pray** for humility and **resolve** to keep following Him.

Further Study

- Scholars often note a significant change from the collection of prophecies in Isaiah 1–39 (with their gloomier tone) to those in Isaiah 40–66 (with their more hopeful tone). In fact, some scholars insist the changes are so great that the two halves of the book couldn't possibly be written by the same guy—but we disagree. After all, one person can have a wide variety of experiences, and the change of tone in Isaiah simply illustrates how God often changes the direction of His followers' lives.

• The word used in the old Greek version of Isaiah 43:5 for "gather" is the same word used in the New Testament for gathering people—as well as crops and fish. In Matthew 13:47, Jesus said, "Again, the kingdom of heaven is like a net that was thrown into the sea and gathered fish of every kind." So Jesus compared the sorting of fish to the sorting of people, separating those who are righteous because of their encounter with Him from those who are not (Matt. 13:1–52; note the parable of the sower that Jesus shared from a boat in 13:1–23, and in 13:14–15 Jesus cited Isa. 6:9–10).

• First-century Jews were expecting a specific fulfillment of Moses's prediction that God would provide a new prophet like him for the people to follow (Deut. 18:15–19) in references to "the Prophet" (John 1:21, 25; 6:14; 7:40) and to "the one who is to come" (Luke 7:18–35; Matt. 11:2 19). Given all this, read the conversation Jesus had on the mountain with Moses and Elijah in Luke 9:28–36. Take note of the several allusions to the OT exodus in the way Luke told the story, in order to show that Jesus is the new exodus leader.

Fun fact: the word for the "departure" that Jesus would lead (Luke 9:31) is literally the Greek word "exodus" (ἔξοδος). And then Jesus brought it all home when He said, "If you believed Moses, you would believe me; for he wrote of me" (John 5:46).

Bible mic drop.

"Bring out the people who are blind, yet have eyes, who are deaf, yet have ears! All the nations gather together, and the peoples assemble. Who among them can declare this, and show us the former things? Let them bring their witnesses to prove them right, and let them hear and say, It is true. 'You are my witnesses,' declares the Lord, 'and my servant whom I have chosen, that you may know and believe me and understand that I am he. Before me no god was formed, nor shall there be any after me.'"

Isaiah 43:8–10

Lesson 5

What Does It Mean to Be Chosen?

YOU ARE A WITNESS

JOHN THE BAPTIST: I thought you were here to ask about miracles.

NICODEMUS: But first I wanted to tell you of a miracle that I've seen but cannot comprehend.

JOHN THE BAPTIST: And then to make accusations.

NICODEMUS: This is pointless. Clearly, you're not a frothing madman, but every bit as unreasonable.

JOHN THE BAPTIST: You imprison me and then accuse me of being ill-tempered about it?

NICODEMUS: I am not your captor. Do you not understand? This is a Roman cell. I came to speak to the warden on your behalf.

JOHN THE BAPTIST: On my behalf? Why are you really here, old man?

NICODEMUS: The official reason? You're a Jewish citizen. If you've broken Jewish law, it sets a dangerous precedent to allow Rome to adjudicate.

JOHN THE BAPTIST: And the real reason?

(Nicodemus retakes a seat on the stool. A thoughtful beat.)

NICODEMUS: The truth? I am far from home, and I am looking in places I would never go because I am searching for an explanation for something I cannot unsee.

> Witness:
> to see, hear, or know through personal experience; to testify; to give or offer evidence of.

Blind Eyes

Many things vie for our attention. We have set goals and five-year plans, opinions and political affiliations, needs and responsibilities, relationships and reputations to maintain, and specific ways we want our lives to unfold. But what we prioritize and pursue tends to also be where we place our hope—hope for happiness, steadiness, wholeness, and the like.

Turns out, there's nothing new under the sun because the people in Jesus's day also had a tendency to misplace hope. In episode 5 of *The Chosen* called "The Wedding Gift," the parents are hoping for a union that will benefit their children and a celebration that will secure their standing in the community. The newlyweds are hoping for a happy, healthy life together full of love and children and fulfilled dreams. The disciples are hoping that Jesus would interrupt the festivities to make His Messianic debut and accelerate their emancipation from Rome. And wedding attendees are hoping for a really good party.

And nothing is wrong with any of it.

Except when any of it intrudes on our ability to see. And then do.

Your Turn

1. What are your main priorities in life? Meaning, what things do you spend the most time and energy pursuing? (No Sunday school answers, please—just honest ones.)

OT Context

We've spent some time talking about the exodus of God's chosen people from Egypt, but the miracles didn't start there. Before Moses found the courage to enter Pharaoh's throne room and demand the release of the Israelites, God met him in the wilderness.

> Now Moses was keeping the flock of his father-in-law, Jethro, the priest of Midian, and he led his flock to the west side of the wilderness … And the angel of the LORD appeared to him in a flame of fire out of the midst of a bush. He looked, and behold, the bush was burning, yet it was not consumed. And Moses said, "I will turn aside to see this great sight, why the bush is not burned." When the LORD saw that he turned aside to see, God called to him out of the bush, "Moses, Moses!" And he said, "Here I am." Then he said, "Do not come near; take your sandals off your feet, for the place on which you are standing is holy ground." And he said, "I am the God of your father, the God of Abraham, the God of Isaac, and the God of Jacob." And Moses hid his face, for he was afraid to look at God.
>
> Then the LORD said, "I have surely seen the affliction of my people who are in Egypt and have heard their cry because of their taskmasters. I know their sufferings, and I have come down to deliver them out of the hand of the Egyptians…. Come, I will send you to Pharaoh that you may bring my people, the children of Israel, out of Egypt." But Moses said to God, "Who am I that I should go to Pharaoh and bring the children of Israel out of Egypt?" [And God] said, "But I will be with you.…"
>
> Then Moses said to God, "If I come to the people of Israel and say to them, 'The God of your fathers has sent me to you,' and they ask me, 'What is his name?' what shall I say to them?" God said to Moses, "I AM WHO I AM." (Ex. 3:1–14)

It was a tall order. The pharaohs of Egypt were not only kings, they were considered to be gods on earth. To stand in front of one and demand anything would've been a death sentence. But Moses had been in the presence of the one true God; he was an eyewitness and couldn't deny what he'd seen or neglect to do what he'd been told.

Moses was called to serve the **King of Kings** and to appeal to Pharaoh on His behalf. "I AM WHO I AM" was the name God gave Himself because it's limitless and because no single word could ever capture the fullness of His character. God is all-powerful, all-knowing, all-seeing—which meant the guy who put Israel in chains was about to face off with the One who could squash him like a bug. And ultimately did.

I AM WHO I AM: this divine name, as it's called, comes from the Hebrew letters equivalent to YHWH, from which we get the English derivative "Jehovah."

Fast-forward about nine centuries when Isaiah was appealing to the nation of Israel on God's behalf: "'You are my witnesses,' declares the LORD, 'and my servant whom I have chosen, that you may know and believe me and understand that I am he. Before me no god was formed, nor shall there be any after me'" (Isa. 43:10).

Time and again Israel had seen God's power on display—in Egypt, through the Red Sea, and into the Promised Land. They'd seen God gather, protect, and provide in the most miraculous ways, **but not for their sake alone.** As witnesses, they were to use their firsthand knowledge to testify to the character and very existence of the one true God—to appeal to the people around them who were worshipping false gods and believing things that weren't true.

That was the endgame, just as it was when Jesus performed miracles.

Your Turn

2. Ten times Pharaoh refused to free the Israelites. So ten times God unleashed plagues upon the land (Ex. 7–11). How was Pharaoh *blind, yet had eyes and deaf, yet had ears* (Isa. 43:8)?

3. In Isaiah 43:8–10, God challenged the people to produce anyone who could prophesy, and then He pointed to the Israelites and said, "You are my witnesses," because they *had experienced* His power to prophesy and bring about and conquer and control. In your opinion, what kind of responsibility comes with that kind of knowledge?

Prophesy: the power to announce in advance what will happen.

4. In ancient times, people worshipped gods made out of "wood and stone, the work of human hands" (Deut. 4:28) as well as people like Pharaoh who made divine claims (though they couldn't back them up). While times and culture have changed, what and who do we worship now instead of the one true God?

See and Tell

> "On the third day there was a wedding at Cana in Galilee, and the mother of Jesus was there. Jesus also was invited to the wedding with his disciples. When the wine ran out, the mother of Jesus said to him, 'They have no wine.'"
>
> John 2:1–3

In Jesus's day, wine was a staple at most meals and a must at every celebration. But at this wedding, the wine had run out—a humiliation of epic proportions for the groom's family who was hosting. Jesus's mother took it upon herself to find Jesus and bring Him up to speed. "They have no wine" were her words, but her sense of urgency was clear—*help*!

Jesus's newly recruited disciples watched as He instructed the servants to fill jars with water. They did as they were told, which included taking a glass of water to the master of the feast. At some point between the drawing and the giving, the water turned into wine. The party and reputation of his friends were saved—and witnesses of Jesus's true identity were born (John 2:6–11).

Mary Magdalene may or may not have been at the wedding, but being rescued from seven demons had more than convinced her who Jesus really was. She'd been delivered from death, so she followed Jesus to His. She was, in fact, one of the few with Him until the very end.

But it wasn't just that initial miracle that secured Mary's allegiance to Jesus; it grew as she followed Him. She listened intently to His teaching, marveled at His compassion, and became fiercely loyal to the One who healed the oppressed and set captives free. The time she spent with Him, along with every subsequent miracle, substantiated what she knew: Jesus was God's Son. So Mary was His witness.

Nicodemus showed glimmers of belief, but we don't know if he ever fully accepted Jesus as Lord. Scripture makes it clear he had an open mind, because he requested a secret meeting with Jesus where he asked a bunch of questions. He obviously didn't want to be like those who are "blind, yet have eyes, who are deaf, yet have ears" (Isa. 43:8) and confessed, "Rabbi, we know that you are a teacher come from God, for no one can do these signs that you do unless God is with him" (John 3:2). But Nicodemus stopped short of knowing and understanding that Jesus is the Son of God—at least in that moment—and there's little more recorded of him in Scripture.

Matthew eventually became a follower of Jesus, even writing an eyewitness account in the NT, the Gospel of Matthew. While we don't know exactly what caused him to abandon his tax booth the moment he was called, we have a pretty good idea from Matthew's own account:

> Getting into a boat [Jesus] crossed over and came to his own city. And behold, some people brought to him a paralytic, lying on a bed. And when Jesus saw their faith, he said to the paralytic, "Take heart, my son; your sins are forgiven." And behold, some of the scribes said to themselves, "This man is blaspheming." But Jesus, knowing their thoughts, said, "Why do you think evil in your hearts? For which is easier, to say, 'Your sins are forgiven,' or to say, 'Rise and walk'? But that you may know that the Son of Man has authority on earth to forgive sins"—he then said to the paralytic—"Rise, pick up your bed and go home." And he rose and went home.…
>
> As Jesus passed on from there, he saw a man called Matthew sitting at the tax booth, and he said to him, "Follow me." And he rose and followed him. (Matt. 9:1–7, 9)

Perhaps Matthew witnessed the miracle that preceded his calling. Perhaps he believed Jesus had the power to forgive his many sins. Whatever the catalyst, Matthew's eyes and

---

Some suggest that Nicodemus's participation in the burial of Jesus hints at his having become a true believer (John 19:39).

ears were opened. When the moment came, he dropped everything to follow Jesus and became a faithful witness for the rest of his life.

Simon also believed what he'd seen and heard, and was likely one of the disciples in attendance at the wedding in Cana. No doubt, witnessing the water change into wine, on top of the miraculous catch of all those fish, confirmed his newfound faith that Jesus was the Messiah. For the next three years, Simon solidified his allegiance to Jesus, along with his willingness to boldly take God's message of salvation to the ends of the earth.

And here's the point: followers of Jesus see, believe, and understand that He's the Son of God, the Savior of the World. Then like Moses, Isaiah, Mary, Matthew, and Simon, they become witnesses in service to the one true King.

Your Turn

5. The first four books of the New Testament are first-century accounts of Jesus's three-year ministry, written by guys who were alive at the time. How does knowing that change the way you read them?

6. To be a witness to is "to see, hear, or know through personal experience." Describe your personal experience with Jesus, and use this moment to testify to your own heart about what He's done for you.

7. The conversation between John the Baptist and Nicodemus in this episode dramatizes Nicodemus's curiosity. He's been seeing things that don't make sense and sincerely investigating. Read Proverbs 30:4 (the verse John quotes in response to Nicodemus), and answer the questions the curious Pharisee couldn't. *Who has ascended to heaven and come down?*

Jesus Is the One True King

Some people say Jesus never claimed to be God—that He was a good man and a powerful teacher, a humanitarian and an example we should follow, but His followers added the "divine" part.

Incorrect. Not only were there witnesses to His miracles (accounts corroborated and recorded by multiple people), He also identified Himself the same way God did to Moses: "Jesus said to them, 'Truly, truly, I say to you, before Abraham was, I am.' So they picked up stones to throw at him" (John 8:58–59). It's not a question of whether or not Jesus claimed to be God—OT context makes it clear that He did, which is why the religious leaders wanted to kill Him.

Rather the question is, do *you* believe Him? And if you do, what kind of responsibility comes with that kind of knowledge? Here's a hint and one last look at our key verse: "'You are my witnesses,' declares the LORD, 'and my servant whom I have chosen, that you may know and believe me and understand that I am he.'"

As God's chosen people, we are to serve the one true King and worship Him alone. And then we are to testify on His behalf—to share our knowledge and experience of God with others. To declare that nothing we do can save us from the consequences of sin. No amount of striving or attaining can satisfy our souls. And no other relationship but the one we have with Jesus can usher us into the kingdom of heaven.

NICODEMUS *(turning to go)*: I should never have come here.

JOHN THE BAPTIST: All your life you've been asleep!

(Nicodemus stops in his tracks, listens without turning around.)

JOHN THE BAPTIST (CONT'D): Make straight the way for the King! He is here to awaken the earth, but some will not want to waken. They're in love with the dark.

I wonder which one you'll be.

Your Turn

8. Even in his search for the truth, Nicodemus remained resistant to it. What are some factors that cause people to resist? In what area(s) of your life and to what degree are you resisting?

9. Read John 10:30–33, 37–39. In spite of the miraculous signs Jesus was doing, some people just didn't believe—some even hated Him. How does knowing Jesus experienced both positive and negative reactions impact your willingness to be a witness for Him?

10. Toward the end of the episode, Jesus says to Thomas, "Come with Me and I'll show you a new way to count and measure. A different way to see time." What does that mean, and how does it impact your priorities?

Prayer Focus

Give thanks to God for the Bible, our written record of history and the testimony of His actions in the world. Give thanks for His intervention in your life and in the lives of those around you. Give thanks for Jesus, God's only Son, who was willing to exercise God's power and love on earth—not for His sake, but for ours. **Ask** God for courage and opportunities to tell others what you've come to know, believe, and understand about Him.

Further Study

- Isaiah refers to the blind and deaf being healed as a picture of God's powerful rescue. In Isaiah 43:8, the same imagery is used to describe stubborn people—those who have the ability to see and hear but refuse to do so. When he was beginning his ministry, Isaiah was warned that many Israelites would indeed refuse to behold God's power and heed His call (Isa. 6:8–10). Interestingly, Jesus referred to the same passage in His ministry as a warning to those who refused to hear His message (Matt. 13:10–17; Mark 4:10–12; Luke 8:9–10; and John 9:39).

- Compare Isaiah 40:3–5 and Luke 3:1–6. John the Baptist embraced his role as a witness, proclaiming the one true King's arrival. He specifically noted, "I am not the Christ.… I am the voice of one crying out in the wilderness, 'Make straight the way of the Lord,' as the prophet Isaiah said" (John 1:20, 23). He also reminded his listeners, "You yourselves bear me witness, that I said, 'I am not the Christ, but I have been sent before him.' The one who has the bride is the bridegroom. The friend of the bridegroom, who stands and hears him, rejoices greatly at the bridegroom's voice. Therefore this joy of mine is now complete. He must increase, but I must decrease" (John 3:28–30).

"'I, I am the LORD, and besides me there is no savior. I declared and saved and proclaimed, when there was no strange god among you; and you are my witnesses,' declares the LORD, 'and I am God. And henceforth I am he; there is none who can deliver from my hand; I work, and who can turn it back?'"

Isaiah 43:11–13

Lesson 6

What Does It Mean to Be Chosen?

YOU ARE MADE NEW

(Mary screams as a man with stringy hair and gaunt features, visibly ravaged by leprosy, stumbles toward the traveling group.)

JOHN: It's a leper. Stay back!

"No strange god" — no false god, no other gods, no idols.

(James and John quickly place themselves between Mary and the leper. Little James covers his mouth with a scarf as the group collectively backs away.)

LITTLE JAMES: Cover your mouths! Don't breathe his air!

(John zealously pulls a large knife from his waistband and brandishes it.)

JOHN: Don't come any closer!

(But Jesus moves toward the leper.)

JESUS: It's okay, John. It's okay.

STONE MASON *(desperately hurling himself facedown before Jesus)*: Please, please.

(Jesus holds up a hand to silence His followers' cries for caution.)

STONE MASON (CONT'D): Please don't turn away from me.

JESUS: I won't.

STONE MASON: Lord, if You are willing, You can make me clean. Only if You want to, I submit to You. My sister, she was a servant at the wedding, she told me what You can do. I know You can heal if You are willing.

(Jesus's face curls up into gut-wrenching compassion. He swallows hard to regain His voice.)

JESUS: I am willing.

(stretching out His hand)

Be cleansed.

Transformation

Sometimes it's easier to come to Jesus than to stay with Jesus. We experience a crisis or need that drives us to Him, but old patterns of behavior reemerge. Bad influences, wrong thinking, past trauma, ongoing urges to sin—a host of things can creep back in, making it hard to believe a new way of living and being is really possible. But it *is* possible.

In episode 6 of *The Chosen*, "Indescribable Compassion," a man suffering from leprosy comes to Jesus in desperate need. In ancient times, leprosy was a vicious condition with no known cure. It deformed its victims by causing lumps as well as scale-like wounds to grow on the body and could even lead to the complete degeneration of skin and twisting of bones. Fingers, toes, ears, and noses sometimes rotted away, making it difficult for people to breathe and likely for them to go blind. Doing the daily work required to survive became nearly impossible.

The modern use of the term *leprosy* is usually limited to Hansen's disease—a slow-growing bacterial infection affecting the nerves, skin, eyes, and nose, which can lead to loss of touch sensation, crippling, paralysis, and blindness. In biblical times, however, the term *leprosy* was inclusive of many different skin conditions.

Those suspected of contracting the disease had to show themselves to the priest, who would evaluate their condition and diagnose them as "clean" or "unclean"—and "unclean" meant you were counted as good as dead and banished from the city to keep the disease from spreading. Lepers were forced to live in tents or caves in designated colonies, wore bells to alert people to their presence, and were required to yell "Unclean! Unclean!" should anyone accidentally come within the legal range. Having been ripped from their homes, families, friends, and all other comforts in life, their only hope for relief was death.

Correction. Death was their only hope apart from Jesus.

Your Turn

1. Like the leper in episode 6, some people have radical come-to-Jesus moments. Others experience change in their lives over time. Regardless of how fast or slow, Jesus always transforms the lives of His followers. What changes has He made in your life? What new things are you hoping still come?

OT Context

The nation of Israel had a staying problem. Over and over in the Old Testament we see them cry out to God in a crisis, only to become unfaithful to Him again once rescued. **But God remained faithful to them**—to the point of overhauling the system.

> Behold, the days are coming, declares the LORD, when I will make a **new covenant** with the house of Israel and the house of Judah, not like the covenant that I made with their fathers on the day when I took them by the hand to bring them out of the land of Egypt, my covenant that they broke, though I was their husband, declares the LORD. For this is the covenant that I will make with the house of Israel after those days, declares the LORD: I will put my law within them, and I will write it on their hearts. And I will be their God, and they shall be my people.... For I will forgive their iniquity, and I will remember their sin no more. (Jer. 31:31–34)

In every new circumstance, God gave Israel the opportunity to be faithful. But instead, they were faithfully *unfaithful* because, as it turns out, mankind is incapable of

The Sin Cycle

God's Plan

We sin   We deviate

We receive   We need to be
forgiveness   rescued

We repent

(Refer to original cycle p. 21)

staying the course. Sooner or later, we go our own way—our sinful, foolish, destructive way. We read about the OT chosen people and marvel at their stupidity. *How could people who experienced Red Sea–sized miracles continually disobey the God who loved them?*

But in reality, we're just like them, because none of us are capable of being good. Not on our own anyway, and certainly not for long. We sin, repent, return, repeat, which means Israel was the living, breathing picture of humanity's desperate need for change.

One that came from the inside out.

Your Turn

Throughout the Old Testament, God revealed His plan of redemption through a series of covenants:

The Abrahamic Covenant	The Mosaic Covenant	The Davidic Covenant	The New Covenant
God promised Abraham and his descendants that they would be a great nation, have a homeland, and be a blessing to the world.	God promised the Israelites that they would participate in the Abrahamic blessings if they loved God and their neighbors, kept His law, and represented Him to the world.	God promised David and the nation of Israel peace and security with a Davidic descendant ruling as king forever.	God promised His people restored lives with His law internalized in their hearts, with profound knowledge of Him, and with their sins forgiven.
Genesis 17:1–21	Exodus 19–24	2 Samuel 7:1–29; 23:5	Jeremiah 31:31–34; Ezekiel 36:26–27

2. The Abrahamic, Davidic, and new covenants were **unconditional**. The Mosaic covenant was **conditional**. In the previous chart, underline what God required of the Israelites in the Mosaic covenant in order to secure His blessings.

3. Read Jeremiah 31:31–34. In the Mosaic covenant, God wrote His law—the Ten Commandments—on two stone tablets (Ex. 34:1; Deut. 10:1–5). In the new covenant, God writes His law on our _____ .

4. Why do you think Israel's persistent failure to keep the Mosaic covenant led to God revealing the new covenant, and what does that tell you about His character?

Covenant:
a formal, solemn, binding agreement.

Unconditional:
absolute, not qualified or limited.

Conditional:
subject to requirements being met.

The Mosaic covenant made clear the need for Jesus to do what we could never do for ourselves. Which means the new covenant was never plan B; it was always plan A.

Jesus = plan A.

Inside Out

"As [Jesus] was teaching, Pharisees and teachers of the law were sitting there.… And behold, some men were bringing on a bed a man who was paralyzed, and they were seeking to bring him in and lay him before Jesus, but finding no way to bring him in, because of the crowd, they went up on the roof and let him down with his bed through the tiles into the midst before Jesus. And when he saw their faith, he said, 'Man, your sins are forgiven you.' And the scribes and the Pharisees began to question, saying, 'Who is this who speaks blasphemies? Who can forgive sins but God alone?' When Jesus perceived their thoughts, he answered them, 'Why do you question in your hearts? Which is easier, to say, "Your sins are forgiven you," or to say, "Rise and walk"? But that you may know that the Son of Man has authority on earth to forgive sins'—he said to the man who was paralyzed—'I say to you, rise, pick up your bed and go home.' And immediately he rose up before them and picked up what he had been lying on and went home, glorifying God."

Luke 5:17–25

People came to Jesus for the miracles, but the miracles weren't the point; healing the body demonstrated Jesus's power and willingness to heal the heart. Up until that moment, teachers of the law believed in the power of the law—they assumed that obeying the Ten Commandments (along with all the other dos and don'ts they piled on) was the way to be forgiven and made new. But the problem with behaving our way to salvation is that we can't do it. We can't *not* sin. In our own strength, we can't keep the law—not perfectly, not completely, not all the time. Like the Israelites, we wander away from the God who loves us. Like the Israelites—including Mary, Nicodemus, Matthew, and Simon—we need an overhaul of the system, one that depends on Jesus's goodness instead of our own.

Mary Magdalene is the quintessential picture of being made new. She was demon possessed and governed by darkness and all the shame and isolation that came with it. She had zero ability to make herself presentable to God. But in an instant, she was healed— her body and heart transformed.

Nicodemus was a teacher of the law, respected and esteemed for his "righteous" behavior and confident in his own wisdom—at least until Jesus came onto the scene. Truth is, attaining and maintaining one's own righteousness would've been an exhausting endeavor, even for a Pharisee. As Nicodemus witnessed the people around him being transformed, he couldn't help but wonder who Jesus really was … though, as Jesus said, the miracles made it pretty clear.

Matthew wasn't the first disciple called. Perhaps he witnessed Jesus's power—the physical transformation of the paralytic and the inward transformations of people like Mary and Simon. Perhaps in spite of his apparent indifference toward others, he was just plain sick of himself. Perhaps Matthew longed to be made new.

Simon also experienced major changes in his heart and life after coming to Jesus— though they weren't all at once. Throughout the NT we continue to see spiritual growth in Simon Peter's life, as he learned a new way of living and being. But the major difference between Simon and religious leaders like Nicodemus was that Simon was no longer trying to be good in his own strength. Instead, he was following Jesus and depending on Him for direction, wisdom, and the ability to remain. He was allowing his relationship with Jesus to fundamentally change him from the inside out.

It's clear (and also reassuring) that our NT brothers and sisters were at different levels of growth regarding their faith in Jesus. Indeed, transformation occurs slowly in some and faster in others, depending on the circumstances or season of life. But Jesus is patient with each of us because He knows that when God *declares and saves and proclaims,* no one can turn it back (Isa. 43:11–13).

Your Turn

5. For many people, a new start is hard to imagine. But what does Psalm 103:10–12 say about God's capacity to forgive and begin again?

6. Which of our four main characters do you relate to most regarding your own transformation? Mary, whose life changed in an instant? Nicodemus, who remained resistant and skeptical, perhaps even unwilling to undergo the changes that would come from following Jesus? Matthew, who was earnest and open, though perhaps a little slower to make the leap? Or Simon, who was all-in early on, but who continued to struggle as he grew in faith?

7. Read John 10:27–30 below, and underline all the claims Jesus makes about (a) Himself and (b) the way He cares for His followers (referred to here as "sheep"):

> My sheep hear my voice, and I know them, and they follow me. I give them eternal life, and they will never perish, and no one will snatch them out of my hand. My Father, who has given them to me, is greater than all, and no one is able to snatch them out of the Father's hand. I and the Father are one.

Jesus Is Our Re-Creator

> "Therefore, if anyone is in Christ, he is a new creation. The old has passed away; behold, the new has come. All this is from God, who through Christ reconciled us to himself … not counting [our] trespasses against [us] … Therefore, we are ambassadors for Christ, God making his appeal [to the world] through us. We implore you on behalf of Christ, be reconciled to God. For our sake he made him to be sin who knew no sin, so that in him we might become the righteousness of God."
>
> 2 Corinthians 5:17–21

Reconciled:
restore friendly relations between; cause to coexist in harmony; to make compatible.

Righteousness:
the quality of being morally right or justifiable.

Jesus did for us what the rules could not do in us. Meaning, the sinless Son of God kept the law of Moses perfectly and therefore had no sin of His own to die for. But in keeping the law, He died for *our* sins in *our* place—He suffered *our* rightful consequence. And so, the law exposes our desperate need for salvation that only comes through faith in Jesus, who is the fulfillment of the law, the prophets, and the covenants.

But then what? Through Jesus we have forgiveness of sins and reconciliation with God (can we get an amen?), but that's not all, because just as God said in Isaiah 43:13, "There is none who can deliver from my hand; I work, and who can turn it back?"

Unlike Israel and the whole wide world, God is faithful to finish what He starts—which means that once we belong to Him, nothing and no one can undo it. While bad influences, past trauma, and sin remain, **so does He**. God never leaves us, never forsakes us (Deut. 31:6). And He continues to work in our hearts and minds as we follow, transforming us from the inside out. Just as He was committed to Israel in spite of her weaknesses and failure, so too does He commit Himself to anyone who believes in the One He has sent.

STONE MASON (*inspecting his beautifully healed hands and arms, turning them over in awe—*): I knew it, I knew it, I knew it. What … what can I ever do …

JESUS (*quietly*): No, do not say anything to anyone.

STONE MASON (*bewildered*): You don't seek Your own honor?

JESUS: Please just do Me this one thing.

STONE MASON: But what do I tell people?

JESUS: Go and show yourself to the priest. Let him inspect you and see that you are cleansed. Make the proper offering in the temple, as Moses commanded. And go on your way.

(*Jesus turns to His followers.*)

JESUS (CONT'D): Who has an extra tunic?

(*Immediately every male disciple starts haphazardly reaching into his bag for any spare garment.*)

JESUS (CONT'D): Just one of you, just one of you. That's enough.

(*Thaddeus emerges, unslinging his rucksack and pulling out an extra cloth.*)

JESUS (*chuckling as He adjusts the fresh new tunic around Stone Mason's shoulders*): Green is definitely your color. Not too shabby.

Your Turn

8. According to 2 Corinthians 5:17–21, what are some of the differences between pre-Jesus living and post-Jesus living, regardless of our ongoing battle with sin?

9. In this episode, Matthew makes an insightful comment: "Conquest is not simply conquering nations, but imposing a new way of life." In what ways does this describe the people Jesus saves?

10. Underline everything that is *declared* and *proclaimed* and *new* in Jesus:

> But now that faith has come, we are no longer under [the law], for in Christ Jesus you are all [children] of God, through faith. For as many of you as were baptized into Christ have put on Christ. There is neither Jew nor Greek, there is neither slave nor free, there is no male and female, for you are all one in Christ Jesus. And if you are Christ's, then you are Abraham's offspring, heirs according to promise. (Gal. 3:25–29)

Prayer Focus

If you're still **evaluating** the evidence of Jesus's indescribable love and have not yet **come to faith** in Him, **ask** God for help to see what's true and to **make the right decision**. If you've already **come to faith** in Jesus, **thank** Him for the new life He has given you, and ask Him to help you **stay the course**.

Further Study

- The idea of being made new is addressed again in Isaiah 43:18–19:

Remember not the former things,
  nor consider the things of old.
Behold, I am doing a new thing,
  now it springs forth, do you not perceive it?

Compare this to 2 Corinthians 5:17–18, where Paul described new life in Jesus:

Therefore, if anyone is in Christ, he is a new creation. The old has passed away; behold, the new has come. All this is from God, who through Christ reconciled us to himself.

- In the healing of the crippled man who was let down through the roof (Mark 2:1–12; Luke 5:17–26), Jesus directly connected His ability to forgive people of their sins with His ability to heal their bodies. Compare this to what God promised Israel in 2 Chronicles 7:14–18. Notice the common themes of forgiving, healing, and declaring.
- God sometimes fulfills His promises in ongoing and increasing ways. In fact, God making things new will reach its climax at the end of history, as described in the book of Revelation. There we find that sin will be completely wiped out and a new heaven and a new earth will be established with God and His chosen ones reunited. In Revelation 21:1–5, God declared again and for the final time, "Behold, I am making all things new."

"Thus says the LORD, your Redeemer, the Holy One of Israel: 'For your sake I send to Babylon and bring them all down as fugitives, even the Chaldeans, in the ships in which they rejoice. I am the LORD, your Holy One, the Creator of Israel, your King.'"

Isaiah 43:14–15

Lesson 7

What Does It Mean to Be Chosen?

YOU ARE ESTABLISHED

(Matthew and his mother sit in awkward silence at a table with clay cups of water.)

MATTHEW: Will Alphaeus be home soon?

ISABEL: He's away on a work trip.

MATTHEW: Where would work take him? Does he no longer make leather goods?

ISABEL: His shop was robbed. Many of the shops have been. Crime is rampant. It makes it very difficult to reopen.

MATTHEW: He loved his shop.

(Matthew takes it all in. Feeling the sting of all the life he's missed.)

ISABEL: But we still have a roof over our heads, which is more than some people can say.

MATTHEW: You can ask me for money if you ever need it.

ISABEL: How can you say that?

MATTHEW: It's quite common. I've seen many parents entirely dependent on—

ISABEL: Your father would sooner die than take your blood money.

MATTHEW: I know you are ashamed of me, but your decision is irrational. Rome will continue to collect taxes no matter what. I'm skilled with numbers—

ISABEL: Did you come here to justify yourself?

MATTHEW: No! *(Matthew stands, frustrated with his inability to communicate.)* Everything's like … sand in a flood. The things I thought I knew to be true …

ISABEL: Are you in trouble?

MATTHEW: Do you think that impossible things can happen? That overturn the laws of nature? That cannot be explained?

ISABEL *(eyes lighting up at a memory)*: That's what people asked when you were a boy. Even the rabbis were astonished at your talent for reading, math, the way you could think faster than any child. They thought you'd be someone great.

MATTHEW *(honestly)*: Great at what? I am rich. I have an armed escort. I am trusted by the Praetor of Galilee—

ISABEL: We never dreamed you would use the talent God gave you to bleed your people dry!

(Matthew studies her face. He knows her words should hurt him, but they don't. His mind goes immediately back to—)

MATTHEW: But have you ever seen anything miraculous?

ISABEL: Matthew—

MATTHEW: My whole world—everything I thought I knew—what if it's wrong?!

ISABEL: I think you should go.

Shifting Sand

We live in an unpredictable world. There are natural disasters, terrorist attacks, car crashes, and cancer. And, as it turns out, global pandemics. While there's definitely order in creation (math, science, patterns, logic), there's also chaos and complexity. For goodness' sake, 80 percent of the ocean on our globe and 96 percent of the visible galaxy beyond remain unexplored—and we know even less about our own brains. We know we have them and that they're amazing, but we don't fully grasp their intricacies and potential or how connections are made and lost.

The truth is that we can't fathom all that God has made, and we certainly can't control it. And that freaks us out. We fear life's apparent instability because we strongly desire the opposite. We want to know our needs will be met. We want to be safe and healthy and know that we'll have enough money to make ends meet. We want to feel solid ground beneath our feet. But in episode 7 called "Invitations," the ground is shifting, and the tax man whose life had been predictable, ordered, clean, and controlled is struggling to make sense of it.

"Everything's like sand in a flood …"

Take heart, Matthew. Because all the things we don't know and can't control point us to the One who **does know** and **can control** and **is**.

Your Turn

1. While faith and reason are not opposites, expressing faith in God invites us to move beyond our own finite levels of human comprehension and control. Can you describe a time when your experience with God invited you to move beyond your own capacity?

OT Context

Through Isaiah, God invited the ancient Israelites to live lives of faith, but they refused. So in 722 BC, the northern kingdom (a.k.a, Israel or Ephraim) was conquered and carried into exile by Assyria. God mercifully spared the southern kingdom (a.k.a, Judah) but warned that if they continued rebelling against Him, it would result in a similar fate. Of course, they persisted in their sinful ways and God made good on what He said.

The rising world power known as Babylonia (whose capital city was Babylon and whose citizens were sometimes called "Chaldeans") eventually conquered the southern kingdom

> Calling the Babylonians "Chaldeans" is somewhat analogous to using "Hoosiers" for people living in Indiana or "Cornhuskers" for people living in Nebraska.

and carried the Israelites away from their homeland in waves of deportations (ca. 605–586 BC). The consequence came a century or so *after* the initial warning from Isaiah but included God's promise to rescue them back.

And now we're all caught up, because the message delivered in Isaiah 43:14–15 is super specific: the Chaldeans would conquer God's people and then become fugitives themselves. The Babylonian sense of security came from their great success in commercial shipping ("the ships in which they rejoice"), but they were powerless against the Creator of the seas.

Isaiah 13:1–14:23 is also about God's judgment on Babylonia and rescuing His people from them.

Isaiah 47 is about the Babylonian/Chaldean humiliation that resulted from their proud, self-confident, unmerciful wickedness (see also Jer. 50–51).

Your Turn

2. What do you think of God using wicked people (like the Babylonians) to punish other wicked people (like the Israelites had been)?

Establish: to set up on a firm or permanent basis.

3. The sin of the Israelites brought about their destruction. But God chose to redeem them again, even announcing His rescue plan through Isaiah more than one hundred years in advance! What does that indicate about God's determination to establish Israel as His people?

4. In Isaiah 43:15, God described Himself with four labels: "I am the LORD, your Holy One, the Creator of Israel, your King." What are the implications of each descriptor?

Sand or Stone

The nation of Israel did what we all do—they tried to establish *themselves*. Meaning, they tried to secure the lives they wanted in their own strength, on their own terms, in their own time. Which only ensured their great big fall.

> "[Jesus said,] 'Everyone then who hears these words of mine and does them will be like a wise man who built his house on the rock. And the rain fell, and the floods came, and the winds blew and beat on that house, but it did not fall, because it had been founded on the rock. And everyone who hears these words of mine and does not do them will be like a foolish man who built his house on the sand. And the rain fell, and the floods came, and the winds blew and beat against that house, and it fell, and great was the fall of it.'"
>
> Matthew 7:24–27

Mary Magdalene's world was a flood until the moment Jesus grabbed hold of her and placed her on the Rock—at which point she began to experience deep-seated peace and purpose for the first time in her entire life. As she followed Jesus, she became more and more secure in His love and acceptance, experiencing firsthand that in Him there's healing of past wounds, stability no matter the circumstances, and hope for a future in heaven.

Nicodemus felt the flood but wasn't ready to abandon his plot of sand. (Not that we know of, anyway.) He'd been waiting and watching for the promised redemption of God to arrive but was having a difficult time relinquishing his preconceived notions of what it would look like—and what it would require him to give up. So at least for the time being, he decided to keep doing life on his own terms and in his own strength.

"It's true, there is a lot you would give up. But what you would gain is far greater and more lasting."

Matthew finally relinquished his flooding beachfront property for holy ground because, unlike Nicodemus (or at least *faster* than Nicodemus), he reached the conclusion that Jesus was indeed the Redeemer they'd been waiting for. And, man, did Matthew need one. Instead of continuing to rely on money, power, and position for security, Matthew turned to Jesus.

Simon Peter stood firmly on the Rock. By the time Jesus came on the scene, Simon was painfully aware of his inability to attain or maintain stability—he'd exhausted his own resources and was desperate, which was why he embraced a new way of life founded on the One who never changes, never fails, and never grows weary. And then Jesus established Simon: "And I tell you, you are Peter, and on this rock I will build my church, and the gates of hell shall not prevail against it" (Matt. 16:18).

Your Turn

5. In what ways have you built your house on the sand? Mind you, even after we make the decision to follow Jesus, we're still capable of sand dwelling.

6. As Nicodemus struggles with the decision to follow Jesus in episode 7, he quotes Psalm 2:12: "Kiss the Son, lest he be angry, and you perish in the way." Indeed, to die in the midst of sin, in the midst of *not* knowing Jesus and *not* being established in Him, would be tragic. But Jesus responds to Nicodemus with the rest of the psalm: "Blessed are all who take refuge in him."

What do you think it means to "take refuge" in Jesus, and how does it relate to His teaching on building your life on the Rock?

7. Simon was skeptical (understatement) of Matthew becoming a Jesus follower. Have you ever been like Simon, somehow thinking it was your right or responsibility to judge other followers of Jesus?

Jesus Is Our Sure Foundation

Jesus doesn't promise that following Him will result in zero storms. On the contrary, He says that *when* storms come, His followers won't fall because they are firmly established. So what does that mean?

- **The Holy Spirit lives in us.** Think about that! God takes up residency in our hearts and minds, which means we're never without His presence, power, love, resources, or wisdom. "I will ask the Father, and he will give you another Helper, to be with you forever, even the Spirit of truth, whom the world cannot receive, because it neither sees him nor knows him. You know him, for he dwells with you and will be in you" (John 14:16–17).

- **Our needs will be met.** When our lives are built on the sure foundation of Jesus Christ, we can trust Him to provide what we need. "Therefore do not be anxious, saying, 'What shall we eat?' or 'What shall we drink?' or 'What shall we wear?' For the Gentiles seek after all these things, and your heavenly Father knows that you need them all. But seek first the kingdom of God and his righteousness, and all these things will be added to you" (Matt. 6:31–33).

- **God will accomplish His purposes.** No matter what happens in our lives or in the world around us, God remains in control. Just as He used the Babylonians to bring about His plan, so too does He continue to work all things for the sake of His kingdom and His chosen people. "Remember this and stand firm, recall it to mind, you transgressors, remember the former things of old; for I am God, and there is no other; I am God, and there is none like me, declaring the end from the beginning and from ancient times things not yet done, saying, 'My counsel shall stand, and I will accomplish all my purpose,' calling a bird of prey from the east, the man of my counsel from a far country. I have spoken, and I will bring it to pass; I have purposed, and I will do it" (Isa. 46:8–11).

And that's just scratching the surface.

The stability and security we long for doesn't come from money, relationships, good health, or even dreams fulfilled, because all of that ebbs and flows. Outward things simply can't be counted on to provide the peace and confidence that come when our foundation is sure. Jesus *is* that sure foundation—the Creator in charge of everything and the One who promises to never leave, forsake, or fail us. That doesn't mean life will always go the way we want it to. In God's wisdom, He sometimes allows hard things. But it does mean that because He's both sovereign and good, He'll use *all the things* for our good and His glory. He'll keep us standing through the storm.

JESUS: Matthew, son of Alphaeus.

(Matthew leans into the light. He locks eyes with Jesus.)

MATTHEW: Yes?

JESUS: Follow Me.

MATTHEW *(registering the command)*: Me?

JESUS *(chuckles)*: Yes, you.

SIMON *(stepping forward to Jesus)*: Whoa, what are You doing?

MATTHEW: You want ME to join You?

GAIUS *(taking a half step forward)*: Keep moving, street preacher.

(Jesus just keeps staring at Matthew, smiling.)

SIMON: Do You have any idea what this guy has done? Do You even know him?

(Matthew looks at Jesus, curious himself about the answer.)

JESUS *(maintaining His gaze)*: Yes.

(In an instant, Matthew's burden, confusion, guilt … all leave him. He looks genuinely happy. He gathers his things.)

GAIUS: Listen—

(Gaius is interrupted by the sound of Matthew unlocking the side door. Matthew exits the booth, tablet under his arm.)

GAIUS (CONT'D): What are you doing?

(Matthew locks the outer door and holds the key out to Gaius. Gaius seizes him by the shirt, tugging him back.)

GAIUS (CONT'D): Where do you think you're going?

MATTHEW: Gaius, let me go.

GAIUS: Have you lost your mind? You have money. Quintus protects you. No Jew lives as good as you. You're gonna throw it all away?

MATTHEW *(wrenching free and smiling)*: Yes.

Your Turn

8. What are the storms in your life?

9. Read Colossians 2:6–7. Explain the difference between knowing about Jesus and being an established believer.

10. Back up for a minute. During the plague of poisonous snakes sent upon the rebellious Israelites, God directed Moses to put a replica snake on a pole and instruct the dying but now repentant Israelites to express their faith in Him by looking to the snake (Num. 21:4–9). It was a picture of the ultimate redemption God would provide through faith in Jesus—if only spiritually dying but repentant people would look to Him. How would looking at Jesus instead of your circumstances change your circumstances?

Prayer Focus

Thank God for His redemptive work in the Old Testament lives of the Israelites, as they pictured the coming Messiah. **Thank** Him for sending Jesus, the ultimate Redeemer, upon whom your life can now be established. **Ask** the Lord for ever-increasing faith to **stay** on firm ground in gratitude to the Holy One, your Creator, your King. **Pray** for someone you know whose house is still on shifting sands.

Further Study

- Read Proverbs 16:1–5 and notice how it treats several of the themes that have been discussed in lesson 7. These include God's control over people's successes, His ability to work even through wicked people, Him having the last word, and the invitation to depend on Him alone for success.

- Even the success Babylonia had in conquering other nations was something God allowed for His own purposes (see the predictions in Isa. 39:5–7 and Jer. 21:1–10 and the fulfillment in 2 Kings 24–25 and 2 Chron. 36:5–21). But the Chaldeans were wicked too (Isa. 47:5–7), and the One in control of all things promised to punish them for their godless pride and redeem a representative remnant of His people from them (Isa. 48:12–22; Hab. 1–3).

- Read 1 Corinthians 10. Compare God's OT warnings for sinful people with Paul's NT warnings for sinful people (in this case, some members of the church in Corinth). Of course, Paul's message is also for us because we're all tempted to do life on our own terms, no matter the century we're born into.

"Thus says the LORD, who makes a way in the sea, a path in the mighty waters, who brings forth chariot and horse, army and warrior; they lie down, they cannot rise, they are extinguished, quenched like a wick: 'Remember not the former things, nor consider the things of old. Behold, I am doing a new thing; now it springs forth, do you not perceive it? I will make a way in the wilderness and rivers in the desert.'"

Isaiah 43:16-19

What Does It Mean to Be Chosen?

YOU ARE CARRIED

ANDREW: What city is that?

MATTHEW: Jezreel. The southernmost town in Galilee. From there we veer east to the Jordan River.

(Jesus breezes past them, going a different direction.)

BIG JAMES: Rabbi, where are You going?

ANDREW: Do You need something?

JESUS: This way, friends!

(They scramble to catch up.)

MATTHEW: I'm sorry, but, uh, the map shows Jezreel is two miles southeast of here and is met by a road east to the Jordan. We need to adjust our course thirty degrees to—

JESUS: We're not going to the Jordan. We're going through Samaria.

(Disbelief ripples through the group.)

ANDREW: Are You telling a joke?

JESUS: There's a place that I want to stop. Plus, it makes our journey shorter by almost half.

MATTHEW: And our odds of violent attack more likely by double.

JESUS: Is that an exact figure?

ANDREW: Forgive me, Teacher, but it's safer to go around Samaria by way of the Jordan in the Decapolis.

JESUS: Did you join Me for safety reasons?

BIG JAMES: But, Rabbi, they're Samaritans.

JESUS: Good observation, Big James. What's your point?

BIG JAMES: Rabbi … these are the people who profaned our temple with the dead bones, they hate us—

JOHN: They fought against us with the Seleucids in the Maccabean wars. I-I've never even spoken to a Samaritan.

JESUS: And we destroyed their temple a hundred years ago. And none of you here were present for any of these things. Listen … if we are going to have a question-and-answer session every time we do something you're not used to, it's going to be a very annoying time together for all of us.

A New Thing

Most of us are wary of new things. Familiarity is comfortable and predictable, whereas change brings the unknown—and the unknown is scary and strange and uncomfortable and unpredictable. But surrendering to Jesus as Lord doesn't leave much room for things to stay the same since He's committed to changing our hearts and lives and also the whole wide world.

In episode 8 of *The Chosen* called "I Am He," the disciples are being introduced to the concept of change. Radical change, in fact. They went from living in houses to pitching tents. From earning their own way to depending on Jesus to show them the way—spiritually and literally—since they were following Him from town to town. From making plans for their lives to having no plan other than serving God for the *rest* of their lives.

So much change would've been debilitatingly scary.

Except for the fact that it wasn't.

Your Turn

1. What new thing are you afraid Jesus might lead you to? (Missionary work, adoption, ending a toxic relationship, sharing your faith, leaving your job—so many terrifying options; feel free to name more than one.)

OT Context

Throughout this study we've referenced the Old Testament story of God rescuing His chosen people from slavery in Egypt. The exodus was such an important part of Israelite history, its memory is often repeated throughout the OT as well as in Sunday school classes and sermons and even on the big screen (though Hollywood has yet to do it justice, but we digress). In fact, seven hundred years after it occurred, Isaiah reminisced about it too: "Thus says the LORD, who makes a way in the sea, a path in the mighty waters, who brings forth chariot and horse, army and warrior; they lie down, they cannot rise, they are extinguished, quenched like a wick … I will make a way in the wilderness and rivers in the desert" (Isa. 43:16–17, 19).

Reminiscing = the plagues, the parting of the Red Sea, God's presence in a cloud by day and fire by night, provision of food and water in the desert, and so on and so forth.

And then God promptly told the people to forget it.

"Remember not the former things, nor consider the things of old. Behold, I am doing a new thing; now it springs forth, do you not perceive it?" (Isa. 43:18–19). Using words that recalled His past rescue, God specifically instructed, "Don't recall that past rescue!"—which seems paradoxical. But He didn't want Israel celebrating their history to the detriment of their future. He didn't want them thinking the God of miracles was a thing of the past. Instead, He was asking them to follow the One who does new things, forges new paths, and carries His chosen people along.

Your Turn

2. Why was it important for the Israelites to be reminded of God's faithfulness in the past? Why was it also important for them not to get stuck there?

3. Read Jeremiah 16:14–15. Isaiah wasn't the only prophet to talk about the Lord doing something new. As the people of Judah were being carried into captivity by the Babylonians, the prophet Jeremiah had a similar message. What new thing did God want His people to be able to say?

4. Throughout the OT, God called people to things that should've been debilitating but weren't, because the people He called He also carried. Guys like Abraham (Gen. 12:1–3), Jacob (Gen. 46:2–4), Moses (Ex. 33:12–17), and David (1 Sam. 17:20–49) were able to do impossible things because God worked through them, making the impossible possible. What impact does their faith *plus God's willingness and ability to carry them* have on your faith journey?

Off-Roading

"And he called the twelve together and gave them power and authority over all demons and to cure diseases, and he sent them out to proclaim the kingdom of God and to heal. And he said to them, 'Take nothing for your journey, no staff, nor bag, nor bread, nor money; and do not have two tunics. And whatever house you enter, stay there, and from there depart. And wherever they do not receive you, when you leave that town shake off the dust from your feet as a testimony against them.' And they departed and went through the villages, preaching the gospel and healing everywhere."

Luke 9:1–6

The New Testament followers of Jesus were on the ground floor of the best new thing, but it required them to look forward, to literally *move* forward, and by doing so, to put their faith into action. Faith that Jesus could be trusted when He gave very specific instructions. Faith that God would indeed provide for their needs as they served Him. Faith that He would continue to teach and grow them spiritually, enabling them to do more than they'd ever thought possible. Faith that the strength of the One who parted the Red Sea would more than compensate for their weaknesses on the journey. Faith that just as God carried the nation of Israel, He would carry them.

There was no other way to make it work. If they wanted to go with Jesus, they had to leave their old way of doing things behind. They had to relinquish control and trust Him to fill in the gaps. And spoiler alert: He did.

Mary Magdalene was a single woman with a traumatic personal history. But she followed Jesus from town to town, trading the familiarity of home for the unknown alongside her Savior—which meant she trusted Jesus not only for her physical well-being but also for her ongoing sanctification. And over time, she became less like her former self and more like the One she was following.

Sanctification: to be made holy (set apart) or righteous.

Nicodemus didn't get to experience the "walking around with Jesus" part—but that doesn't mean he never trusted Him as Lord. Oh, what a relief it would've been for our beloved Pharisee, so concerned with adhering to the law and being "good," to fall into the strong arms of his Redeemer. To be carried by the only One capable of true goodness, of restoring desperate hearts, and of leading God's chosen to the Promised Land of heaven.

Matthew must've experienced a moment of pause when Jesus gave very specific, very terrifying marching orders. The disciples were sent into the countryside to do what they'd seen Him do, without food or shelter. They were instructed to go with nothing but the shirts on their backs. Boiled down, the plan was "take nothing because you'll be provided for in your moment of need." For a guy like Matthew, who had once loved the security of money more than people, it was no doubt a testing of his faith.

But Jesus's power carried him along.

Simon's self-sufficiency would've made being carried a foreign, maybe even unattractive, concept. Plenty of times throughout the New Testament, we see him attempt to follow the Messiah in his own strength—only to fumble and fail—but Jesus persisted because learning to depend on Him was wholly necessary if Simon was going to participate in kingdom building. And by Jesus's grace and in His strength, Simon Peter did just that:

> And more than ever believers were added to the Lord, multitudes of both men and women, so that they even carried out the sick into the streets and laid them on cots and mats, that as Peter came by at least his shadow might fall on some of them. The people also gathered from the towns around Jerusalem, bringing the sick and those afflicted with unclean spirits, and they were all healed. (Acts 5:14–16)

The early disciples knew better than anyone that the power given to them was from Jesus. Apart from Him, they could do nothing, because Jesus made the way.

Your Turn

5. The disciples were asked to travel throughout the region, telling people about Jesus with no provisions of their own. What do you imagine your response to Jesus would be if He asked the same of you?

6. What kinds of things do you think Nicodemus missed out on by *not* following when others did? Like him, in what ways are you trying to do life in your own strength and in your own way?

7. Read Isaiah 46:3–4. God explicitly told His chosen people that He would carry them all the days of their lives. Knowing about His past miracles and hearing His vow to remain with His chosen people, how should these verses inspire you moving forward?

Jesus Is Our Waymaker

Jesus doesn't ask us to make our own way. He asks us to allow *Him* to lead and equip and provide. Yet it often still feels like so much is required of us—because, in truth, so much is. Like His early followers, we have to put our faith in Jesus and follow Him with our whole hearts, which can be hard since it means giving up our own plans and goals, along with all the predictability and familiarity they offer. But also like His early followers, **on our own we can do nothing.** Correction. What we *can* do is surrender and follow where Jesus leads. He's the One actually doing all the things, including fundamentally changing us from the inside out.

> "For consider your calling, brothers [and sisters]: not many of you were wise according to worldly standards, not many were powerful, not many were of noble birth. But God chose what is foolish in the world to shame the wise; God chose what is weak in the world to shame the strong; God chose what is low and despised in the world, even things that are not, to bring to nothing things that are, so that no human being might boast in the presence of God. And because of him you are in Christ Jesus, who became to us wisdom from God, righteousness and sanctification and redemption, so that, as it is written, 'Let the one who boasts, boast in the Lord.'"
>
> 1 Corinthians 1:26–31

Just as God made a way through the wilderness and rivers through the desert in Old Testament days, and just as Jesus made the lame to walk and the blind to see in the New, so too is He still making the way. Indeed, the God of miracles is not a thing of the past; He's doing new things in and through us, building His kingdom and accomplishing His good and perfect will—from the beginning of time to the end. Nothing is too big for Him to handle, which means nothing is too big for those of us who are in His care. We belong to the living God, and we are carried by His Son.

PHOTINA: You picked the wrong person.

JESUS: I came to Samaria just to meet you. Do you think it's an accident I'm here in the middle of the day?

PHOTINA: I am rejected by others.

JESUS: I know. But not by the Messiah.

PHOTINA: And you know these things because You are the Christ?

(Jesus nods.)

PHOTINA (CONT'D) *(through tears)*: I'm going to tell everyone.

JESUS: I was counting on it.

(She backs away, not breaking her gaze with Jesus.)

PHOTINA: Spirit and truth?

JESUS: Spirit and truth.

PHOTINA: It won't be all about mountains or temples?

JESUS *(nodding)*: Soon. Just the heart.

PHOTINA: You promise?

JESUS: I promise.

(The disciples arrive from town with food. They stop abruptly and take in the scene: Jesus and this woman standing at a distance facing each other. She turns to run and then sees them.)

PHOTINA *(shouting)*: This man told me everything I've done! Oh—He must be the Christ!

(They stare. Mary smiles. Photina takes off running.)

ANDREW: Hey wait!

BIG JAMES: Your water!

JOHN: You forgot your—

(But she doesn't hear. In the distance we hear her shouting.)

PHOTINA: Come see a man who told me everything I ever did!

(Jesus laughs beautifully as He watches her run.)

LITTLE JAMES: Rabbi, we got food. What would You like?

JESUS: Ah, I have food to eat you do not know about.

ANDREW: Who got You food?

SIMON: Wait a minute. You told her? And she can tell others?

THADDEUS: What food?

JESUS: My food is to do the will of Him who sent Me and to accomplish His work.

SIMON: You told her who You are?

(Jesus looks at Simon, smirks, and nods.)

SIMON (CONT'D): So does that mean …

JESUS: It means we're going to stay here for a couple days. It's been a long time of sowing, but the fields are ripe for harvest.

SIMON: And so it's time?

JESUS: Let's go.

Your Turn

8. Make a list of anything you can't currently see your way through, then go back through your list and write Jesus's corresponding attributes from this study—attributes that are bigger and more powerful than what's too big for you. (Jesus is our Rescuer, Provider, Keeper, Leader, King, Re-Creator, Sure Foundation, and Waymaker.)

9. Read Hebrews 12:1–3. Explain what it means for Jesus to be the "founder and perfecter" of your faith.

10. What tangible thing might God be calling you to say or do in order to put your faith into action?

Prayer Focus

Thank God for His promise to keep and carry His chosen people. **Ask** Jesus, the founder and perfecter of your faith, to **continue changing** you from the inside out, making you more like Him every day. **Ask** for opportunities to **do hard things** in His name and in His power—the same power that parted the Red Sea. **Praise** Him for allowing you to be a part of building His kingdom, just like those who've gone before you.

Further Study

- Psalm 106 is a celebration song of the OT Israelites about God's persistent love (106:1–5) and specifically mentions that God chose them in spite of their unworthiness, their stubborn disobedience, and their imperfect, intermittent faith (106:6–43). In all this, the exodus experience stands as the ideal model of God's rescuing work, and Moses is specifically called God's "chosen one" to serve as the deliverer of the Israelites (106:23). The psalm closes by once again celebrating God's faithfulness to carry (106:44–48)—which is fulfilled in Jesus.

- In Luke 9:28–36, Jesus had a transfiguration experience that three of His disciples witnessed, in which He talked with Moses and Elijah about the upcoming departure He would accomplish in Jerusalem (the Greek word for "departure" is *exodus*—see the connection?!). At the close of the conversation, God spoke from a cloud, telling the followers, "This is my Son, my Chosen One; listen to him!" (9:35). When the cloud lifted, the OT heroes of the faith were gone, and Jesus was found alone (9:36).

So ... that was intense.

• Jesus's ascension in Acts 1:9–11 might've felt a little familiar to the three disciples who had witnessed the transfiguration—Jesus being covered in a cloud and some heavenly figures showing up. However, instead of Jesus remaining on earth as He had in Luke 9, His ascension in Acts 1 signaled His departure for heaven, and His chosen ones remained behind. But Jesus had prepared them for His departure and promised His continued presence through the Holy Spirit, or Helper (Acts 1:4–8; John 14:15–17, 25–29; 16:7–15). Note in particular Acts 1:8, "But you will receive power when the Holy Spirit has come upon you, and you will be my witnesses in Jerusalem and in all Judea and Samaria, and to the end of the earth." A few days later, Jesus's followers indeed received His power by way of the Spirit, which enabled them to continue on even after He ascended to heaven. Which meant they were not left alone; they were prepared and sent and carried.

"The wild beasts will honor me, the jackals and the ostriches, for I give water in the wilderness, rivers in the desert, to give drink to my chosen people, the people whom I formed for myself that they might declare my praise."

Isaiah 43:20–21

Conclusion

What Does It Mean to Be Chosen?

YOU ARE A VESSEL OF PRAISE

Why study a passage from the book of Isaiah in the Old Testament when the life of Jesus is covered in the New Testament? Well, after spending eight weeks learning about the history of God's relationship with His chosen people (our spiritual forerunners, for better or worse), as well as God's continued faithfulness to His chosen people through Jesus and up to the present day, the answer seems a little more obvious than it did at the start:

Because God deserves it.

And because we're preserved by it.

Israel's propensity to wander, along with all the consequences they endured as a result, is like a giant flashing light for the rest of us—a warning for us to stay close to the God of our salvation. We shake our heads at Israel's foolishness and hardness of heart, but we're just like them. We're ridiculous and sin-soaked, easily led astray, broken, self-centered, and in desperate need of saving. But also just like them, we're called by the One whose relentless love and faithfulness have made a way for us to return and be restored. And to stay.

Oh, that we would, because He's so, so good.

"As [Jesus] was drawing near ... the whole multitude of his disciples began to rejoice and praise God with a loud voice for all the mighty works that they had seen, saying, 'Blessed is the King who comes in the name of the Lord! Peace in heaven and glory in the highest!'

And some of the Pharisees in the crowd said to him, 'Teacher, rebuke your disciples.'

He answered, 'I tell you, if these were silent, the very stones would cry out'" (Luke 19:37–40).

... and also wild beasts and jackals and ostriches, because if the people won't praise, the rest of creation will!

He's worthy of our praise.

God is patient. "The Lord is not slow to fulfill his promise as some count slowness, but is patient toward you, not wishing that any should perish, but that all should reach repentance" (2 Pet. 3:9).

Trespasses: sin.

God is merciful. "But God, being rich in mercy, because of the great love with which he loved us, even when we were dead in our trespasses, made us alive together with Christ—by grace you have been saved—" (Eph. 2:4–5).

God is generous. "—and [God] raised us up with him and seated us with him in the heavenly places in Christ Jesus, so that in the coming ages he might show the immeasurable riches of his grace in kindness toward us in Christ Jesus" (Eph. 2:6–7).

God is just. "The times of ignorance God overlooked, but now he commands all people everywhere to repent, because he has fixed a day on which he will judge the world in righteousness by a man [Jesus] whom he has appointed; and of this he has given assurance to all by raising him from the dead" (Acts 17:30–31).

Propitiation: the atoning sacrifice of Christ that satisfies God's wrath against sin and removes our guilt.

God is love. "In this the love of God was made manifest among us, that God sent his only Son into the world, so that we might live through him. In this is love, not that we have loved God but that he loved us and sent his Son to be the propitiation for our sins" (1 John 4:9–10).

God's goodness and worthiness to be worshipped have been put on full display in His actions toward His chosen people—from creation until right now. In the Old Testament, He pursued Israel through prophets like Isaiah and through miracles like the Red Sea—all of which point to Jesus, who is the *ultimate* proof of God's love, because in order to bring us to Himself, He gave Himself.

How could we *not* praise Him?

We were formed for God "that [we] might declare [His] praise" (Isa. 43:21). That's our purpose! All other earthly pursuits are incapable of satisfying because we're wired to praise; it's in our spiritual DNA. We're made to commune with God, designed to be fulfilled by Him alone and to glorify Him alone. And through Jesus and the power of His indwelling Holy Spirit—*and because of who He is*—we're given a new identity, becoming more like Jesus and less like the *was* we once were.

We are called because He's our Rescuer.

We rest because He's Present.

We are cherished because He's our Keeper.

We change course because He's our Leader.

We are witnesses because He's our King.

We are made new because He's our Re-Creator.

We are established because He's our Sure Foundation.

We are carried because He's our Waymaker.

We are vessels of praise because He's Worthy.

We are chosen.

NOTES

NOTES

NOTES

NOTES

NOTES

ABOUT THE AUTHORS

Amanda Jenkins is an author, speaker, and mother of four. She has written six books, including *Confessions of a Raging Perfectionist*, a memoir that has inspired women's Bible studies and conferences around the country. She specializes in writing and teaching raw authenticity in our faith, and she is the lead creator for *The Chosen*'s extra content, including *The Chosen* devotionals, volumes I and II, and the children's book *The Chosen: Jesus Loves the Little Children*. She lives just outside of Chicago with her children and husband, Dallas, creator of *The Chosen*.

Dallas Jenkins is a filmmaker, author, speaker, and father of four. Over the past twenty years, he has directed and produced over a dozen films for companies such as Warner Brothers, Lionsgate, Universal Studios, and Hallmark Channel. He is now the creator of *The Chosen*, the first-ever multi-season show about the life of Christ and the highest crowd-funded media project of all-time. He is also the coauthor of the bestselling *Chosen* devotional books.

The official evangelical biblical consultant for *The Chosen* TV series, **Douglas S. Huffman** (PhD, Trinity Evangelical Divinity School) is Professor of New Testament and Associate Dean of Biblical and Theological Studies at Talbot School of Theology (Biola University) in California. Specializing in New Testament Greek, Luke–Acts, and Christian Thought, he is the author of *Verbal Aspect Theory and the Prohibitions in the Greek New Testament* and *The Handy Guide to New Testament Greek*; contributing editor of such books as *God Under Fire: Modern Scholarship Reinvents God, How Then Should We Choose?: Three Views on God's Will and Decision Making,* and *Christian Contours: How a Biblical Worldview Shapes the Mind and Heart*; and contributor to several theological journals and reference works. Dr. Huffman can be seen on *The Chosen*'s "Bible Roundtables" on *The Chosen* app. He enjoys working with Biola undergraduate students, pointing them to Scripture as God's Word for us today.